THE Children's Media YEARBOOK 2022

The Children's Media
FOUNDATION

The Children's Media Yearbook is a publication of The Children's Media Foundation

Director, Greg Childs

Administrator, Jacqui Wells

The Children's Media Foundation

15 Briarbank Rd

London

W13 0HH

info@thechildrensmediafoundation.org

First published 2022

Cover and book design by Rebekkah Hughes

ISBN 978-1-9161353-2-1

The Children's Media
FOUNDATION

Contents

Editors' Foreword

Hannie Kirkham, Research Manager, Oriel Square and **Dr Ashley Woodfall**, Senior Principal Academic, Bournemouth University

Welcome to the 10th issue of *The Children's Media Yearbook*, published by The Children's Media Foundation (CMF). The *Yearbook* is a unique space, bringing together the voices of those that create media for children, those that research in the field and those that advocate or develop policy for children – as well as the voices of children and young people themselves. As an annual publication the *Yearbook* acts as a 'book of record' of key issues and developments within children's media.

A core aim of the CMF is to stimulate quality debate and the *Yearbook* sits at the heart of this, with the ambition that this debate ultimately informs and impacts productively on children's media and the lives of children.

Within such an active and seemingly ever-changing field, it is impossible to capture all debates, or all sides of a debate, but we have looked to engage with and encourage a plurality of voices. We are very thankful for the time and insight offered by all the contributors and to those who helped us pull the *Yearbook* together – not least Rebekkah Hughes at Oriel Square for the design. As well as airing the challenges facing children's media, the *Yearbook* highlights the creativity, passion and resolve of our community.

This year, like the last, has been turbulent. Beyond the impact of Covid, there have been significant funding, structural and strategy announcements that we are collectively still trying to understand and respond to.

The *Yearbook*, however, starts in a celebratory fashion, with this being an edition of many anniversaries. The biggest and perhaps most obvious is the BBC's centenary. Máire Messenger Davies provides a personal reflection on the place of children's content within the BBC, one formed around a seemingly continual 'fight' for its shape and validity. We also celebrate the 50th anniversaries of *Newsround* (Cynthia Carter) and *Record Breakers* (Joe Godwin), highlighting the importance of moulding content for our audience, as well as the fun of making it.

Nigel Pickard reflects on the 20th anniversary of CBBC and CBeebies. As we go to press, we are still digesting the announcement that CBBC will soon be online only, giving Nigel's piece new significance. There are congratulations aimed overseas as well, as Sebastian Debertin discusses the 25th anniversary of the German public service broadcasting children's channel, KiKA. Children's PSB in Germany offers an interesting comparison to the UK model. Of course, it's also 50 years since *Sesame Street* came to our shores, and David Kleeman offers a round-up of the show's achievements in the meantime.

A perhaps less-known anniversary is that of the All-Party Parliamentary Group for Children's

Media and the Arts, which turns 10 this year. Jayne Kirkham tells of its beginnings and the ways the APPG continues the fight for children's media. As we turn to policy, Colin Ward summarises the CMF-led report on the future of public service media for children, and Jeanette Steemers discusses the demise of the Young Audiences Content Fund and the BBC's strategy for children's content.

We also look at ways to bring policy and research into practice, with guidance on making digital media products and services 'Playful by Design' (Sonia Livingstone and Kruakae Pothong) and recommendations for changes to the Online Safety Bill (Izzy Wicks). We are very pleased to include voices from our audience. Katie Battersby and Rebecca Stringer present a snapshot of how young people consume and think about their favourite content; Rachel Ramsay shares what young people think and feel about today's 'big issues', before we hear from global *Change Makers* about what would have the biggest positive impact on their communities (Gemma Robinson).

The Metaverse was a recurring topic when developing this edition, and we have several contributions about defining it (Japhat Asher), whether or not we should be scared of it (Andy Phippen), how children might interact with it (Jane Movoa) and some words of caution around it's possible effects on mental health (Sonia Livingstone).

From here we move to look at diversity and social mobility. Jo Claessen shows how BBC's *Tiny Happy People* campaign uses film to improve early literacy and engage parents in play, and Margaret Bartley tells how the *Lit in Colour*

campaign is bringing new playwrights to the fore for young people in schools. Mel Rodrigues and Jessica Schibli discuss ways that the industry can improve inclusive representation within itself, and the ways in which it can influence, encourage and enable all young people.

We hear from Genevieve Margrett about how the industry is also looking to better its sustainability, and we have two case studies from sustainable productions (Andrew Snowdon, and Gráinne McGuiness and Gavin Halpin). Gary Pope explores why we need to embed sustainable practices throughout all our work and set the best example for our audience. Peter Stanely-Ward also offers a view of the future with virtual production, which holds so much promise for sustainability.

Maddie Moate and Greg Foot explore other novel means of production, describing their lockdown adventures and getting *Let's Go Live* back on the road. Cecilia Persson also tells of another studio on the move – the transformation of BBC Studios Kids & Family.

In the spirit of sharing practical industry advice, Paul Boross shares his experience on delivering the best pitch. And similarly, Jayne Kirkham offers her wisdom about the craft of adaptation.

Finally, we end with more celebrations, though they are imbued with sadness. The last year has seen the passing of three tremendous people within our industry, and here we pay tribute to them: Rick Jones, Theresa Plummer-Andrews and David McKee.

One last word of thanks for all the contributors to the *Yearbook*. Happy reading!

Industry Under Pressure – Audience Under Threat

Anna Home OBE, Chair, The Children's Media Foundation

In my article for last year's *Yearbook* I ended on an optimistic note. The Young Audiences Content Fund (YACF) was clearly making good progress despite production problems associated with the pandemic.

However, earlier this year the fund was closed in a somewhat peremptory fashion. The announcement came before the end of the fund's three-year pilot and ahead of any evaluation – which was unexpected[1]. The Children's Media Foundation (CMF) and other organisations made strong protests about this decision. We wrote to and had meetings with the Department for Digital, Culture, Media and Sport (DCMS) to convey this was illogical and damaging to the children's media industry.

Assessment of the first two years of YACF operation shows:

- 55 new projects commissioned
- 144 development grants issued
- The commercial Public Service Broadcasters returning to children's commissioning
- An increase in indigenous language production
- Involvement of new companies and producers
- Focus on the nations and regions.

The fund was moving things in the right direction. It had the potential to redress the market failure in children's commissioning revealed by Ofcom in 2017, and much else besides, including some of the government's 'levelling up' agenda and, of course, significant additional provision for UK kids under severe pressure since the start of the lockdowns.

In the last few months it has become clear the decision is final. After the April publication of the white paper *Up Next*[2] – the government's vision for broadcasting in the future – the YACF has become part of a wider discussion about the potential of contestable funding to support public service more broadly in the future.

CMF is pleased that the success of the children's pilot will be taken seriously, but we need to be wary that if a multi-genre contestable fund is introduced in the future, children's content will not end up at the bottom of the list – as was so often the case in the past.

The white paper will dominate discussion in the coming year. It will consider among other things the future of both the BBC and Channel 4. The privatisation of the latter appears to be a fait accompli as far as the Secretary of State is concerned. And that is despite 96% of the respondents to the government's consultation being against it.

Despite its commitment to support the young teen audience, Channel 4 did little to address the under-served 12+ age range. But CMF believes that it can and should appeal to this group, who deserve content geared specifically to their needs – that gives them a voice. We oppose privatisation as it will inevitably lead to the dilution (or disappearance) of public service commitment at Channel 4.

The CMF multi-authored report *Our Children's Future: Does Public Service Media Matter?*[3] explored radical solutions to public service engagement with young people, but it also stressed the crucial importance of the BBC to ensure continued provision of public service content for the young, now and in the foreseeable future. The white paper announces a review of the future of the licence fee which will start this summer and conclude before the end of the current BBC charter in 2027. The government's position is that the licence fee should be abolished. Until we know what the alternatives are, we cannot agree. However, we welcome the debate, and would draw attention to some of the alternatives discussed in *Our Children's Future*. CMF's main concern is protecting the role played by the BBC as the major provider of public service content for children in the UK.

Freezing the licence fee until 2024 is effectively a reduction in funding and already means

there will be programme cuts across the board, including Children's. A decision by Ofcom in May, agreeing to a reduction in CBBC hours of original production in favour of increased acquisition, is also a concern. It inevitably means more international animation and less live-action commissioning. CMF appreciates this is deemed necessary to re-attract the audience that has defected to the streamers and YouTube. But it creates a disturbing precedent and is a trend we will be watching very carefully.

The debate around the white paper will give a once-in-a-generation opportunity to influence the future and to ensure that UK kids and teens get the media they need and deserve. CMF will do as much as we can to achieve a positive outcome for the young audience.

At the end of May there was a radical announcement by BBC Director General Tim Davie that the CBBC channel would no longer be part of the BBC's portfolio of channels. Along with BBC Four it is to become an online-only operation at some point in the next six years. This is in part a reflection of budget cuts, and addresses the concerns Ofcom expressed, that children are migrating away from linear television to on-demand services. The CMF understands this is a future-focused decision, and supports the need to reconnect with the audience lost to on-demand services. However, many details need to be addressed before it happens – not least the lack of ubiquitous high-speed broadband, meaning that some less well-off young people may be excluded from the promised CBBC content onBBC iPlayer. iPlayer is also a problem, as it isn't a natural destination for children and its child-friendly features were all abandoned some time ago as being too costly to maintain. To address

7–12 year olds where they are, and to recapture the 'lost audience', will require smart thinking and significant marketing budgets, to ensure that CBBC content is delivered on multiple platforms, backed by social media activity, and truly available on the online spaces children frequent.

These and other issues will be discussed at CMF-produced sessions at the Children's Media Conference and in further events we'll organise over the months ahead.

We are a relatively small, mainly volunteer organisation, but I believe we fight above our weight. I would like to thank everyone who has been involved in our activities in this busy year and will be involved over the coming months: the CMF Board, Executive Group and the core team led by Greg Childs and Colin Ward. And my thanks to our patrons and supporters who keep us afloat – join us if you want to help make a difference.

[1] https://www.gov.uk/government/publications/up-next-the-governments-vision-for-the-broadcasting-sector. Professor Jeanette Steemers' article describes the demise of the YACF in more detail.

[2] https://www.gov.uk/government/publications/up-next-the-governments-vision-for-the-broadcasting-sector

[3] The challenges of pulling the Public Service Media report together is explored in Colin Ward's article.

Photo: by Ben Wicks on Unsplash

The Children's Media Foundation – Effective Advocacy in a Time of Change

Greg Childs OBE, Director, The Children's Media Foundation

As the children's media industry gathers again in its familiar haunts for the return of the Children's Media Conference (CMC) to Sheffield, I'm reminded that a year ago the Children's Media Foundation (CMF) launched our report into the future of public service media for young people, *Our Children's Future: Does Public Service Media Matter?*[1], and distributed it to all the attendees of Virtual CMC 2021.

Ofcom had just completed its study into the future of public service *Small Screen: Big Debate*[2] and submitted its recommendations to government. The starting gun had been fired and a range of consultations, proposals and, finally, legislation has followed.

The CMF public service media report helped us crystalise our policy position. This is the set of principles we apply to proposals for change in the public service media space. Our policy covers the short, medium and long term:

1. We support the BBC as a publicly funded body. While accepting that the licence fee is flawed and needs reform, subscription is not a viable basis for public service broadcasting. We reject the privatisation of Channel 4 as inevitably leading to abandoning public service commitment.

2. We oppose the closure of the Young Audiences Content Fund (YACF). There is market failure in the kids' television sector and the industry needs the 'shot in the arm' the YACF offers to keep public service content for young people, varied, plural and relevant.

3. Longer term we believe the YACF represents a useful model and testing ground for more radical ways of funding, commissioning and distributing public service content in general. Young people lead the way in their migration to a multiplicity of services – social, streaming, interactive and self-generated – that tell us where public service content needs to be in the not-too-distant future. The YACF is a ready-made body that could pilot new ways of commissioning and funding so that public service content can reach the 'lost' younger audience where they are, rather than where broadcasters think they should be.

We also emphasise one other important recurring theme in the Public Service Media Report – listening to kids. We have criticised Ofcom and the Department for Digital, Culture, Media and

Sport (DCMS) for their failure to sufficiently take into account the changed behaviours and attitudes of young people. The Foundation might itself be guilty of not keeping in touch with young people, so this has stimulated the second phase of the Public Service Media Campaign – Listening to Kids.

As the decision-making on the futures of Channel 4, the BBC and public service in general plays out over the next few years we will contribute research to inform the debate. Partnering with research agencies and academics, we will attempt to uncover how young people think and feel, what matters to them, how they build their world-picture, opinions and attitudes, how this might impact on where or what they watch and, from all of that, what purposes and meaning public service content could and should have for them in the future. It's long-term work and inevitably slower than we would like: as a mainly volunteer-based organisation we lack time and the funds to commission the research as we try to keep up with the public consultations and inquiries around the future of public service media that have now culminated in the government's Broadcasting white paper.

Listening to Kids will be brought to public attention through events. The outcomes of our first research partnership with Dubit, summarised in Dr Rachel Ramsey's 'State of the Nation' *Yearbook* piece, was presented at the 10th anniversary celebration for the All-Party Parliamentary Group for Children's Media and the Arts in November 2021. The APPG is still going strong, under co-chairs Baroness Benjamin and Julie Elliott MP and the deft secretariat provided by CMF's Jayne Kirkham.

Then in April 2022, our second research partnership, *Listening to Kids - Young Voices on Media Choices*[3], featured video-based research by Kids Know Best. More events and more research partnerships will follow into 2023. We are listening at last.

The ideas in the public service media report are also being explored in a series of follow-on events. The first of these considered various ways of funding new approaches to children's and youth media. Inevitably called *Show Me The Money*[4], it featured industry strategists debating the relative value of licence fee-style public funding, levies, lottery grants and other methods of supporting public service content in the future.

This event-based approach to contributing to the public debate will continue at CMC in July 2022 with CMF producing the annual *Question Time* session exploring all the policy issues facing the kids' media industry and through the *CMC Debate,* which will consider 'What Next' – after the closure of the Young Audiences Content Fund.

The YACF and its future have been the major preoccupation of the Foundation in the last six months. On news of its closure at the end of its three-year pilot, CMF swung into action in ways that have become our hallmark. Acting as an 'honest broker', CMF facilitated a campaign coalition of producers, academics, and industry bodies which delivered an open letter to the Secretary of State demanding the YACF's reinstatement[5].

Gathering over 1,000 signatures, the letter led to a meeting with the Minister for Media and the Creative industries, Julia Lopez MP, in May. The minister showed sympathy and enthusiasm for the value that children's media brings to the audience and the economy, but there was no budging on the lack of money available to help. However, subsequent comments by the Secretary of State at a Commons Select Committee hearing indicate that conversations are starting to take place about 'doing something' about kids' content provision. We have also been invited to participate in the evaluation process and thinking ahead to new models of public service. CMF's 'constant tapping' seems to have had some effect – and maybe kids will be listened to after all.

If that is the case, then it's down to our continued advocacy – as the only body representing children's and teen interests in the corridors of media power. And that is the product of the commitment of so many who help what we do.

Our supporters and patrons – and I'd urge you to become one – enable us through their donations to keep going. This year we have been fortunate to welcome Frank Cottrell Boyce and Sir Phil and Lady Alexis Redmond as Lifetime Patrons and, along with the continuing support of companies in the children's media industry

we have been able to successfully keep the All-Party Parliamentary Group active beyond its tenth anniversary, to fund the Public Service Media Report, stage free public events and produce this *Yearbook* once more.

Our lobbying and campaign activity have grown in their effectiveness – thanks to the often unsung work of people in the CMF Executive Group. Numerous questions were asked in Parliament about the loss of the YACF – many of them briefed by our team. And due to the arrival of some new members we can now turn our minds to supporting the 5Rights organisation in its work to ensure that the Online Safety Bill before Parliament will be truly effective in protecting, but also enabling, young people[6].

As CMF Chair Anna Home makes clear in her introductory article for this Yearbook, we are facing unprecedented strains on the children's media industry in the UK. This will impact on the range and quality of content young people can watch. With your help and the help of our dedicated volunteers the Children's Media Foundation will continue the struggle. It's what our young people deserve.

[1] https://www.thechildrensmediafoundation.org/wp-content/uploads/2021/11/PSMR-REPORT-WEB.pdf. Colin Ward's article describes the Public Service Media Report in more detail.

[2] https://www.smallscreenbigdebate.co.uk

[3] https://www.thechildrensmediafoundation.org/events/listening-to-kids-young-voices-on-media-choices

[4] https://www.thechildrensmediafoundation.org/events/show-me-the-money

[5] https://www.thechildrensmediafoundation.org/the-young-audiences-content-fund-campaign. The demise of the YAFC is discussed in Prof Jeanette Steemer's article.

[6] The 5Rights amendments to the Online Safety Bill are detailed in the *Yearbook*'s 'The Children's Sector Speaking as One Voice on the Online Safety Bill' article.

What Next 2.2

The Children's Media Conference is the annual gathering of professionals engaged in communicating to and entertaining kids and young people in the UK, Ireland and beyond.

CMC is a proud supporter of the Children's Media Foundation and pleased to be able to distribute the Children's Media Yearbook to all our CMC 2022 delegates.

Follow, join and chat to us on:
Twitter_@childmediaconf
email_contact@thechildrensmediaconference.com
web_www.thechildrensmediaconference.com

Authors'
Licensing and
Collecting
Society

We support, champion and fight for authors

At ALCS we value writers for the impact they have on our lives, every single day.

That's why we work hard to protect copyright, author's rights, and vital revenue streams for creators. We also pay authors the royalties for secondary uses of their works. To date, we've paid out £600m and boast over 116,000 members worldwide.

Join now  alcs.co.uk

"It's Them There Algorithms": Then and Now in Children's Media, a Personal Reflection as the BBC Turns 100

Dr Máire Messenger Davies, Emerita Professor of Media Studies at Ulster University and Visiting Professor at the University of South Wales

Sorting through some old documents, I came across a copy of the BBC's former broadcasting magazine, *The Listener*, from March 3rd 1977, which included a TV review I had written about children's programmes. What did I review? *The Flumps*, a preschool animation with puppets; *Take Hart*, a how-to art programme with the great Tony Hart; *It's Our Turn*, a show made by and for teenagers; *Heads and Tails*, a musical show about animals with Derek Griffiths; *The Muppet Show, Doctor Who* (both still with us) and a thrilling ITV sci-fi drama, *Children of the Stones*. All these are genres that still survive today but, in other respects, this picture of 1977 children's screen consumption seems almost from another planet.

My review gave a snapshot of what was then a common way of families consuming TV: "Every Monday for the past seven weeks we have huddled together on the couch shivering deliciously at *Children of the Stones* (Harlech, ITV)." This was date viewing, only available once a week, everyone watching together because there was only one other alternative, the BBC's children's offering at the same time, 5pm. Fast forward 45 years and those shivering children, now very grown up, are sharing their current experiences of their own children's screen consumption in a Facebook discussion about kids' viewing habits. One parent posts: "My kids won't watch TV, only YouTube. Only *Newsround* because they watch it at school." Another says: "My eldest loves his YouTubers which quite frankly baffles the hell out of me" and yet another comments: "Their genre of choice is mostly watching YouTube channels of other people playing computer games (yeah, me neither)." One praises YouTube phenomena like *Ryan's World*, beloved by her six year old daughter. When asked about how their children find their favourite YouTube content, she proposed: "It's mainly them there algorithms."

So what has happened here? According to Ofcom's most recent report on children's media consumption[1]: "The trend we have seen in recent years, for children to watch TV content on paid-for on-demand services rather than on live or broadcast TV, has continued. Almost eight in ten children (78%) aged 3–17 watched content on services such as Netflix, Amazon Prime Video and Disney+, compared to less than half (47%) who said they watched live TV."

The 100th anniversary of the BBC has given me the chance to look back over the history of the BBC's children's programmes particularly and children's media generally, in the last few decades. This history not only includes landmark programmes, such as *Newsround*, currently celebrating its 50th anniversary, and still valued by those Facebook posters, but also the technological and policy changes that have affected everything that programme makers were and are trying to do for kids. The years since 1977 have also been a pretty eventful period in my own career; writing for *The Listener* put me in touch with the children's department at the BBC, who helped me when I embarked on a PhD in 1980, studying how children learn from television. This led eventually to an academic career – a career that has included many interesting and happy collaborations with people working in children's television.

In her account of British children's television, published in 1993, Anna Home used the word 'fight' to describe the challenges facing the industry, and this has proved apposite in looking at the history. Home writes about the travails of the BBC's children's department with the arrival of ITV in 1956 and the loss of the BBC's children's audiences to the likes of *Robin Hood*. Within the BBC there was the takeover of the Children's department by Family, and Children's Drama by Adult Drama in 1963–4. There were rows about innovative and controversial drama – *Grange Hill* in 1978. There was a period of creative competition between BBC and ITV in the 1980s, which produced some terrific shows: ITV gave us *Children's Ward* and *The Tomorrow People*, the BBC gave us *Grange Hill*, *Byker Grove* and regular adaptations of children's books. And then came a 1988 White Paper, preparing for the 1990 Broadcasting Act, with its threat of deregulation and a proposal that ITV's commercial companies should no longer be required to provide for children.

The 'fight' for children's content in UK media has never been the sole prerogative of the people who make it, such as producers and writers. In the run-up to the 1990 Act, under the auspices of the Education Department at the British Film Institute, a group called British Action for Children's Television (BACTV) was set up to campaign for children's provision to be included as a

[1] https://www.ofcom.org.uk/research-and-data/media-literacy-research/childrens

protected category in the new arrangements for ITV in the Act. The group included producers such as Anne Wood of Ragdoll Productions, Anna Home, then head of BBC Children's, and Lewis Rudd at ITV; educators such as myself and members of the public; it was chaired by Philip Simpson, head of BFI Education. BACTV, supported by the BFI, organised a huge conference in London in 1989 called *Children and Television: What's going on?* at which the keynote speaker was Angela Rumbold, Minister for Education and Science. At the conference there was a warning from another speaker, Peggy Charren, founder of the American campaign group Action for Children's Television: "Don't go the way of children's television in the US; what you have in the UK is a model for children's provision around the world. Keep it!" The same year, my book, *Television is Good for Your Kids*, based on my PhD research, was published. That helped the cause by getting a lot of scandalised publicity because – let's face it – the prevailing wisdom was that television was terrible for kids. Had this been in the era of clickbait, a book daring to say TV was good for kids would have got me into trouble on the internet. As it was, it got some useful mainstream media coverage.

Photo: by PJ Gal-Szabo on Unsplash

BACTV helped to persuade the government to amend the 1990 Broadcasting Act to include kids' programmes in their requirements for the commercial companies to get a licence. A memorable campaign event was a trip to the House of Commons where we showed MPs examples of current children's drama including the death of Danny Kendall from *Grange Hill*. They had absolutely no idea that this kind of challenging, powerful material was being made for young people. As Sandie Hastie, producer of *Press Gang* (ITV) put it: "We operated under the radar and got away with ground-breaking material about e.g. child abuse because nobody actually noticed what we were doing" (Davies, 2001). Politically, of course, being under the radar has drawbacks – you have to get powerful people to notice what children's producers are doing if the necessary political and funding arrangements are to be made. Hence CMF's current campaign to promote children's media.

A recent heated Facebook discussion about the CBeebies World Cup revealed that the public is also still invested deeply in what their children watch. When it was announced that *Hey Duggee* was the World Cup winner, with *Bluey* in second place, one dad (and a lot of dads got involved in this) challenged: "Anyone up for an argument about this? Obviously, *Bluey* should be No 1 and *Twirlywoos* and *DipDap* should be a good deal higher . . . And no *Go-Jetters* is an absolute *. . .* schoolboy error." The thread went on for pages.

Photo: courtesy of Máire Messenger Davies

"Flumps": gentle humour

The 1990s were a good period for drama and other children's material, but BACTV dispersed for a variety of professional and personal reasons and its archive and functions were eventually taken over by the Voice of the Listener and Viewer (VLV) which had been established in 1983 by the redoubtable Jocelyn Hay; VLV continues to champion public service broadcasting generally, and children's interests in particular. Also in the 1990s, the Children's World Summit movement began in Australia in 1995, producing a Children's Television Charter. The charter stresses the importance of indigenous, home-grown media material because "children should hear, see and express themselves, their culture, their language and their life experiences through TV programs which affirm their sense of self, community and place."

But the 'fight' had to continue. In 2003 came another UK Broadcasting Act in which the protections for children's content in the 1990 Act ceased. In 2006 – when the multichannel digital revolution was well under way, with commercial channels for children multiplying and a ban on 'junk food' advertising during children's viewing hours, ITV ceased children's production, although the CITV channel was launched in 2006, with some original local production. In response to ITV's action, Save Kids' TV was set up, becoming the Children's Media Foundation in 2011. Further changes in programming came when, in 2007, the BBC redefined the child audience as 12 and under. No more *Grange Hill* pregnancy and drugs storylines. In 2012 BBC Children's was moved completely from broadcast to digital and the new channels, CBeebies and CBBC became their only provision for children.

That's a lot of technological and political upheaval. A look at the main kids' schedules now – currently there are 16 children's channels on my smart TV alone – compared with the single channel when the BBC's children's offer started in 1946, shows the extensive structural changes that have overtaken this sector of broadcasting and its audiences. But interestingly, the kinds of genres I noted in 1977 – how-to programmes, drama, documentary, cartoons, music, news – do continue. The Young Audiences Content Fund, championed by the CMF, enabled innovative material for children to be produced for channels other than the BBC, such as the sustainable craft show *Makeaway Takeaway* (CITV) and *The World According to Grandpa* (Milkshake!, Channel 5), but unfortunately the fund has been discontinued. To save it is another ongoing campaign by the CMF. The fight continues.

As well as reflecting on the past in this article, I was asked to predict the future of children's media, so, as is my wont, I decided to turn the question round and ask the audience. The following social media comments aren't representative but may be revealing. What will kids' screen behaviour, including TV, be like in the future?

> M (8) said "I think it'll be how it is now but no live channels – just picking whatever you want when you want it. But I think Saturday night will stay family TV but there'll be special Friday night family shows too."

> L (10) has similar predictions of the future of television – more "pick and choose" TV like Netflix, but still with a sense that "telly will still be physically with us."

And drama retains its power:

> B (9) watches back-to-back episodes of *The Dumping Ground* on BBC iPlayer on a laptop. Says her mother: "She is learning a huge amount about relationships, difference, bullying, families, how to resolve disputes etc etc. She is utterly addicted to it."

I had a similar experience watching *The Demon Headmaster* (CBBC, 2019) on iPlayer with my 10 year old granddaughter. She'd seen it before, but insisted on watching it all the way through again with me; it was a fascinating intergenerational moment when Terence Hardiman as the original TV Demon Headmaster, from the 1990s, finally appeared at the end. A true shivery experience – shared by three generations!

> S (6) is a fan of many YouTube influencers but likes to watch TV too. She says confidently: "Television will be pretty much the same as it is now."

I hope it will be pretty much the same, too. I still huddle together on the sofa, now with my grandchildren; we may be watching *Encanto* on Disney+, we may be sharing a YouTube video, we may be working our way, yet again, through *The Demon Headmaster*; or we'll all be laughing at *Bluey* or being craftily inspired by *Makeaway Takeaway*. I also fear that 'fighting' for good children's media will still be necessary in the future, but I want to be optimistic and say that I think our next generation will be up for it.

Stop press: just as this article was being finalised, the news broke that the BBC is proposing to axe CBBC and move it online for the next three years. (And then what?) This is dreadful news and begs a lot of questions including whether or not there was any meaningful consultation about this decision and what the evidence is that the UK's child audience, which the BBC has a duty to serve, will be better served online than with its own channel. I hope the CMF, the All-Party Parliamentary Group for Children's Media and the Arts and other groups such as the Voice of the Listener and Viewer will question and challenge this decision.

References

Davies, M. M. (1989) *Television is Good for Your Kids*. London: Hilary Shipman.

Davies, M. M. (2001) *Dear BBC: Children, Television Storytelling and the Public Sphere*. Cambridge: Cambridge University Press.

Home, A. (1993) *Into the Box of Delights: A History of Children's Television*. London: BBC Books.

Newsround at 50

Dr Cynthia Carter, Reader in the Cardiff School of Journalism, Media and Culture, Cardiff University

Happy Birthday, *Newsround*! For many, it may seem hard to believe that it has now been a half century since the bulletin was first aired on BBC One. On Tuesday 4th April 1972, at 5.20pm, John Craven, who until then had worked as a reporter for BBC Points West in Bristol, made television history as presenter of one of the world's first children's news programmes.

Initially titled *John Craven's Newsround*, to make it seem more personal and inviting for children, the programme quickly grew in popularity with its audience. It came to be, partly, because Edward Barnes, then deputy head of BBC Children's TV, had a six minute slot to fill on Tuesdays and Thursdays at 5pm (Craven cited in Pelley, 2022). Barnes decided to fill it by creating a news programme for children, an ideal opportunity for the BBC to fulfil its Reithian promise to inform, educate and entertain young audiences. Craven and the others who helped launch *Newsround* strongly felt that children deserved to be informed about what was going on in the world in ways they would find interesting and accessible, thus addressing the Corporation's commitment to children's civic engagement (Messenger Davies et al., 2014).

Photo: Newsround, 1987

The first three decades

Throughout the first twenty years of its broadcast, *Newsround* attracted sizeable audiences, which grew into millions at its height of popularity in the 1980s. From the start, *Newsround* was widely regarded as providing a newscast that took children seriously as a news audience, including stories from adult news as well as those of particular interest to children, such as school, bullying, music, sport, animals, environment, delivered in 'child-friendly' language. In the days before 24-hour rolling news, let alone the internet, some may find it remarkable that, on occasion, *Newsround* actually broke some stories first, such as the news of the assassination attempt of Pope John Paul III in 1981 and the explosion of the space shuttle Challenger in 1986. The programme's strong journalistic team did not hold back on reporting the day's events for its young audience but did, of course, convey them in a way that was understandable and reassuring.

Photo: by CDC on Unsplash

Aside from providing clear and trustworthy news, over the years *Newsround* broke new ground in a number of different ways. For example, it challenged some television news conventions well before most adult news television broadcasters by moving the presenter from behind a desk to sit upon it or to stand; it moved from the presenter being a man wearing a suit and tie to Craven's famous, and much loved, colourful shirts and jumpers.

It was an early champion of diversity amongst its presenters, too, with the first British Asian woman to front its news bulletin, Lucy Mathen, who joined in 1976. Looking back at her career at *Newsround,* Mathen recently remarked: "We found the right language and visuals to report even the most difficult stories, without patronising our audience. It turned out this was what many adult viewers wanted too. Some of my greatest fans were pub landlords, who made sure that they tuned in at 5pm before opening up" (cited in Pelley, 2022). "The makers of *Newsround* were much more aware of the need to reflect the audience, for kids to see people who look like them," remarks Krishnan Guru-Murthy, "and that also meaning bringing in younger presenters" (cited in Wollaston, G2 2022: 3).

Photo: Jim on Flickr

After Craven left in 1989, the 1990s saw *Newsround* expand its reporting team. It was therefore able to offer a number of opportunities for young journalists to gain experience before some would move on to become well-known reporters in adult news. Many had watched the programme in childhood and recall how this experience helped them to develop a deep interest in the engaging with the news and in becoming a journalist – such as

Photo: by Isabella and Zsa Fischer on Unsplash

Julie Etchingham (ITV News), Krishnan Guru-Murthy (Channel 4 News), and Lizo Mzimba (BBC News), to name only a few.

Newsround was also an early advocate of including environmental news well before it became a routine feature of adult news. Guru-Murthy noted that "Kids were interested in the world, in animals, the environment, in saving the planet. We were making programmes about that agenda because that's where kids were already. It's not about adults deciding what children should be interested in; this was the BBC meeting a need that was out there already" (cited in Wollaston, 2022: G2, 2).

Inclusion of these young presenters and reporters marked a shift in *Newsround*'s mode of address to its child audience, from Craven as the steady and trustworthy uncle to one that was more like an older sister and brother who was fun, approachable and yet also serious. There was a livelier, more inviting set with a sofa, rather than a background newsroom, eye-catching graphics, and more frequent scheduling.

The 1990s also saw a number of format changes to the programme, whilst its length and early evening scheduling remained quite stable. Between 1992 and 2012, the *Press Pack* (a journalism club) was a regular feature encouraging children to engage with news by writing a story for the TV bulletin or website.

21st century children's news

An interactive website was launched in 2001, one of the first of its kind in the world (Levell, 2001), along with message boards enabling children to speak to each other about different topics covered by *Newsround*, including one that was dedicated to focused discussion on the news. However, the message boards were abandoned in 2011 due, in part, to the legal and logistical challenges of moderation of postings (Carter 2007).

In assessing these developments at the time, *Newsround* felt rather removed and increasingly remote from its audience, something that it is only now recovering in part, with the reintroduction of features such as the *Press Pack* on 4th April 2022, for instance, and greater engagement with the audience through *Newsround* increasingly eliciting responses to news items on its website – some stories have a 'Comments' button where children can express their views.

From 2013, *Newsround* moved from mainstream channel BBC One to children's digital channel, CBBC, and bulletins were reduced to 3–5 minutes. Past presenter Krishnan Guru-Murthy, now a Channel 4 news anchor, was concerned that shorter bulletins were "too brief for detailed reporting on major stories," which had been "one of the show's strengths" (as cited in Marsden, 2012). CBBC Director, Joe Godwin, said at the time:

> CBBC is the place the vast majority of kids in the UK tune into to watch *Newsround* and their other favourite children's shows. So, it feels for us the right time to stop the regular blocks of children's programming on BBC One and Two (cited in Marsden, 2012).

However, the move ghettoised the bulletin and audiences began to steadily decline (Blackall, 2019; Table 1). In July 2020, Ofcom's acceptance of *Newsround*'s submission to reduce its television broadcast hours to focus on its digital provision due to falling broadcast numbers, saw the eventual axing of the early evening bulletin, and a reduction to the current schedule (May 2022) of just one 8-minute bulletin on CBBC, at 7.45am Monday to Friday, a 10-minute bulletin at 7.40am on Saturday and 5 minutes at 7.40am on Sunday, then watchable throughout the day on *Newsround*'s website. As Waterston (2020) notes, Ofcom's decision has, in effect, allowed *Newsround* to establish the iPlayer as its central delivery platform, in conjunction with the website.

Some journalists at *Newsround* became concerned the changes might lead to "reduced visibility for the programme, as many children come to the site by searching for episodes they have seen at school." Another concern, of course, is that such a change might lead to disengagement with *Newsround* for some segments of its target audience of 8–12 year olds, particularly those who are not sufficiently digitally literate or whose families cannot afford the technology needed to access some of its digital content. Expressing concern about the move to digital platforms, *Newsround* presenter Ricky Boleto stated that although "audiences are changing, and the way young kids watch TV is moving fast […] I worry that as we chase the clicks, we lose focus on what really matters" (cited in Blackall, 2019).

Also criticising the move to digital, former *Newsround* editor Sinead Rocks commented:

> *Newsround* needs more prominence – not less. The ability to watch with parents/families is also important. Relying mainly on a child's ability and interest to seek it out online is short-sighted and sad (cited in Blackall, 2019).

As with the move from BBC One to CBBC in 2012, the shift towards online provision in 2020 (slightly delayed due to the pandemic lockdowns of 2020 and 2021 when *Newsround* increased its provision on television and online) appears to have been motivated more by technology and market-driven changes than understanding the needs and interests of child audiences, whom they presume to know, often with little or no consultation (Carter, Steemers and Messenger Davies, 2021).

Photo: by CDC on Unsplash

The here, now and future of children's news

Journalist Warren Nettleford (2021), who co-developed with media producer Seth Goolnik a daily news programme for young people during the 2019 General Election, argues that the desire to reach young news audiences through technology has not been accompanied by other changes he deems necessary to attract young people to the news. Specifically, the tone of news delivery to this audience is still too top down, where journalists have decided what audiences 'should' know. Instead, he advocates a shift toward delivering news that is "useful, interesting and fun," relayed with humour, but without preaching or an attempt to get down with the kids by "crowbarring youth acronyms into content" (2021, 70). Even though in his view it makes sense to provide news through social media, that doesn't mean simply replicating television or website content on these sites. Instead, there is a need to "build a whole new grammar of highly concentrated storytelling, using everything from eye catching graphics to split screens" – which to my ear sounds remarkably similar to what *Newsround* has been doing for decades with its television bulletin. Nettleford thinks it would be a mistake to assume young audiences want 'woke' ideas and activism combined and delivered to them in the hope it will attract them to the news. This is because, in his view, young people already get a lot of preachy content online and are therefore looking for trustworthy news "to explain how they can personally make a difference" (2021, 70).

This last point brings us squarely back to what *Newsround* has done so well over its half century of providing news for its young audience; helping them understand and engage with the world. At the core of *Newsround*'s success has been its ability to connect with its audience, to be widely regarded as a trusted and reliable provider of news and place core values at the heart of its mission to serve children in their development as young citizens. As Nettleford argues, "news content has moved from the place which is well regulated to a space without the values and identity that have defined broadcasting for generations" (2021, 72).

If public service news for children is central in society, it is important for government to understand where children fit into the digital news world and what policymakers and regulators can do to ensure young people get the highest quality, most trustworthy and engaging news possible. Given the ongoing importance of *Newsround* as one of the few UK providers of news content for children, it should be a collective social duty to see that it thrives and survives, and that the commitment to public service news content for children grows.

An increasing commercial orientation at CBBC saw the March 2021 incorporation of BBC Children's in-house production into BBC Studios, where the Kids & Family team will be competing with commercial broadcasters while at the same time trying to fulfil its commitments to public service broadcasting with CBBC and CBeebies. As great as *Newsround* has been over the past 50 years, it needs to be joined by others with a public service commitment to ensure the future health of trusted news provision for children.

Back to the future

Given there are so many sources of news now available to young people, is *Newsround* still relevant for today's children? Yes, claims current *Newsround* editor Lewis James (Kahn, 2022), who has said that "*Newsround* is as important today as it was in 1972 and plays a significant role in children's lives." Whilst I emphatically agree, I do have some reservations about *Newsround*'s recent direction of digital travel and whether or not, as Nettleford (2021) points out, there is a real commitment by current policymakers, Ofcom and the BBC to ensure the central relationship between these stakeholders and today's and tomorrow's children to ensure they get the news they deserve as young citizens.

"Fifty years on, with children asking questions about war and their need for a trustworthy, sensitive source of news, *Newsround* is more important than ever" (Wollaston, 2022). With these concerns in mind, it may be fitting to give the final word to Craven marking the 50th anniversary, concluding that "Newsround's success proves that children are interested in the world around them, especially if it's explained in ways they can grasp. This is even more important now, when there is so much dangerously false information on social media" (cited in Pelley, 2022: 9).

References

Blackall, M. (2019) BBC plans to drop afternoon Newsround as children go online. *The Guardian*, November 16.

Carter, C. (2007) Talking about my Generation: A Critical Examination of Children's BBC *Newsround* Web Site Discussions about War, Conflict and Terrorism. In Lemish, D. and Götz, M. (eds) *Children and Media in Times of War and Conflict*. Creskill: Hampton Press, 121–142.

Carter, C., Steemers, J. and Messenger Davies, M. (2021) Why Children's News Matters. The Case of CBBC *Newsround*. In *Communications: European Journalism of Communication Research*, 46 (3), 352–372.

Davies, M., Carter, C., Allan, S., and Mendes, K. (2014) News, Children and Citizenship: User-Generated Content and the BBC's *Newsround* Website. In Thornham, H. and Popple, S. (eds) *Content Cultures: Transformations of User Generated Content in Public Service Broadcasting*, London: IB Taurus, (15–36).

Kahn, E. (2022) Newsround Preps Daily British Sign Language Bulletin. *Broadcast*, April 1.

Levell, T. (2001) *Welcome to our site!* Newsround - BBC News. November 16.

Marsden, S. (2012) *BBC Newsround changes criticised by Channel 4 News presenter Krishnan Guru-Murthy*. December 21.

Nettleford, W. (2021) Public Service News for Young People: Where Next? In C. Ward (ed), *Our Children's Future: Does Public Service Media Matter?* London: Children's Media Foundation, 68–73.

Pelley, R. (2022) 'Some of our greatest fans were pub landlords' – how we made Newsround. *The Guardian*, March 28.

Waterston, J. (2020) BBC Axes Evening Edition of Newsround After 48 Years. *The Guardian*, July 28.

The Record Breakers: Fifty Years On

Joe Godwin, Trainee Assistant Producer on *Record Breakers* 1989, Assistant Producer 1990–1991 and Director of BBC Children's 2009–2014

On December 15th 1972, at a quarter past five, the very first episode of *The Record Breakers* was broadcast across most of the UK (viewers in Wales had "their own programmes," in the continuity parlance of the time). The *Radio Times* described it thus:

> Introduced by Roy Castle with Ross and Norris McWhirter who discover the fastest - slowest - strongest - highest - toughest - anyone or anything that claims to be a record breaker. New records will be attempted. Existing records may be broken. Famous old records will be reconstructed. This week's special guest: Dr Roger Bannister, CBE the world's first 4-minute miler.

The first of an eventual 276 programmes, it was originally billed as <u>*The*</u> *Record Breakers*, the definite article lasting until series 12 in 1983 when the programme became plain *Record Breakers*.

I didn't actually get to see the early series – we didn't have a TV, as my dad said we watched too much and sent it back to Radio Rentals. I'm not sure what might astound a young reader more – that people routinely rented their televisions in the seventies or that a children's programme could attract an audience of more than seven million viewers? But millions did tune into *The Record Breakers*.

Record Breakers emerged from *Blue Peter*, where producer Alan Russell and the McWhirter brothers had often overseen record attempts. Roy Castle was already hugely famous – he'd been a star of the West End, Broadway and television since the 1950s. "Our versatile friend from England" had entertained Frank Sinatra at the Sands Hotel Las Vegas. In 1965 Roy played The Doctor's assistant opposite Peter Cushing in the film version of *Dr Who* and, four years before *Record Breakers*, he'd starred as Captain Keene in the classic *Carry On Up the Khyber*. Such was Roy's popularity and versatility that in 1975 he stood in for an unwell Bruce Forsyth on BBC One's *Generation Game* – the biggest light entertainment show of the era.

Roy didn't just talk about records; he broke them himself. In that first series he set a tap dancing record of 24 taps per second, and went on to break many more including the world's longest wing-walk, of which more later.

In spite of not having a TV for part of my childhood – or maybe because of? – I'd grown up with an obsession with working for the BBC. In 1986 I wangled a job at BBC Southampton as a floor manager-cum-graphics operator on *South Today*. In the summer of 1989, I found myself heading off to meet a man called Greg Childs. Greg was the actual Producer of the actual *Record Breakers*, and I had secured a nine-month secondment as a Trainee Assistant Producer. That journey from Southampton to meet Greg was the start of my twenty-five-year adventure in children's media.

But that's enough about me – for a mo. The *Record Breakers* of 1989 was well-resourced. Though nominally a 'factual' programme within Eric Rowan's serious Factual unit, it appeared to have the budget and manners of a light entertainment show. This may have been because it occupied the same slot as *Crackerjack*. Whatever the reason, it was ambitious, professional and definitely showbiz.

1989 was the twilight of a BBC that would disappear under the Producer Choice reforms of the nineties. Children's programmes in the eighties were 'allocated' available in-house resources, which meant the camera crews and heads of department we worked with might have been working on primetime BBC One light entertainment or drama the week before. *Record Breakers* in 1989 was crafted by the best craftspeople in the BBC.

Cheryl Baker got to *Record Breakers* two years before me in 1987, six years after she helped the UK regain its Eurovision pride. She presented the show for 10 years, continuing after Roy's death in 1994. She sums up the experience as "fun, excitement, laughter." Her favourite memories were of an East-to-West trip across America, sweeping up record breakers along the way, the highlight of which was Cheryl's interview with Bob Hope.

I asked Cheryl of her memories of working with Roy: "An absolute joy. He was the consummate professional. He had a great sense of humour, so generous with his time and wisdom – I was privileged to work with him." *Record Breakers* regularly had halfwit trainees like me thrust upon it, but Roy was never anything but kind, helpful, appreciative and respectful.

He was so famous and so popular that, whether it was the world's longest line of pennies on the Isle of Man or the 20th anniversary of Disneyworld in Florida, trying to move through a public place with Roy was impossible.

Photos: courtesy of Joe Godwin

Everyone knew Roy and everyone wanted to chat to him. If he was trying to work and a persistent chatter wouldn't stop, the only clue we ever got that he'd nearly had enough was if he called them 'Pal', at which point we'd usher him away.

The only time I remember him not being recognised was when he, producer Adrian Mills and I were in Dublin to film the world's biggest game of musical chairs. He took being mistaken for TV impressionist Mike Yarwood whilst being pursued down the street in his usual friendly stride. It was also the only time I remember us going on a filming trip and returning with nothing to show; instead of the 10,000 expected musical chairs players, mere dozens turned up, and me and Adrian returned home to face Greg's wrath – we hadn't even got enough bodies or footage for a passable 'heroic failure' film.

Record Breakers opened my eyes to the world. I went to America for the first time with Roy to film at Disneyworld, to Spain with Cheryl to watch the *Guinness Book of Records* being printed, and Longleat, where the Marquis showed me and Roy his collection of 'private collectables.' In Germany Roy and I went to interview Martina Navratilova who, despite months of letters and faxes and middle-of-the-night calls with her agent in the US, didn't know we were coming. After she'd interrupted her tennis tournament to do an interview no one had told her was happening, I asked if I could have a photo with my idol. She grabbed my arm with a vice-like grip and said "you're joking right?" She relented, and that photo remains one of my prized possessions.

In 1990 one of the many records that Roy broke on the show was the world's longest wing walk – three hours and twenty-three minutes – from London to Paris. I had gone ahead to a small airport in Paris to film Cheryl greeting Roy as he landed. Roy's plane took off successfully and headed towards the South coast. But as the camera crew's chase plane attempted to take off, its undercarriage collapsed. Roy flew off towards the Channel with only the mute fixed mini cameras filming him. Producer Greg and Cheryl were sat on an Air France plane waiting to take off for Paris to get ahead of Roy and greet him as he landed. But as the chase plane had blocked the runway, Greg and Cheryl couldn't leave. Nor could thousands of other travellers. I was in Paris, oblivious of all this: there were no mobile phones then.

In the end the runway was cleared, another chase plane was found and, having closed the UK's second busiest airport for several hours, the camera crew caught up with Roy over the Channel. Cheryl and Greg got to Paris in the nick of time and me and my French crew captured her greeting his landing. The experience combined everything that made working on *Record Breakers* so exciting and challenging; huge ambition, complex logistics, incredible teamwork, enormous risks, and always breathing down our necks, the risk of absolute failure or worse.

I earned my first ever nickname during my time on *Record Breakers*. In those days, most show recordings were followed by 'hospitality', usually in some beige conference room in the basement of Television Centre. Room B209, I think. Peanuts and public service plonk. I was so shy, easily embarrassed and therefore awkward and not good at chit chat, especially with famous people, that Cheryl's lovely sister Sheila bestowed upon me the moniker by, which Cheryl still addresses me to this day – Jolly Joe.

Why did so many people watch *Record Breakers* for so many years? Cheryl thinks that its appeal was as a family show that everyone could watch together, in the best traditions of primetime light entertainment.

Alistair McGown, writing on the BFI's website, sums up the show's legacy nicely: "Thirty series is not quite a record in children's television, but certainly shows dedication." *Record Breakers* quietly disappeared in 2001.

Twenty years after I started on *Record Breakers*, I had the honour of becoming Director of BBC Children's. My journey from obsessive wannabee to captain of the ship was complete. But through all the adventures of those years, from Saturday morning TV, children's presentation, a stint at Nickelodeon, and onwards towards Salford, whenever old lags gather and the wine flows, nothing can ever top the excitement, the camaraderie, the camp theatrics or the place in the nation's heart of *Record Breakers*.

Cheryl, Greg Childs and Joe Godwin

"You're joking, right?" Joe meets his idol, Martina Navratilova.

Photos: courtesy of Joe Godwin

Roy Castle's record-breaking wing walk

20 Years of CBeebies and CBBC: Nigel Pickard Discusses the Launch and Legacy

Nigel Pickard, Creative Director, Nevision

Nigel Pickard was Controller of BBC Children's 2000–2003. Here he discusses with Ashley Woodfall his time overseeing the creation and launch of the CBeebies and CBBC channels.

I came from ITV, from the commercial sector, to the BBC for the first time ever in 2000. I joined at a time of liberal upheaval. It was an exciting time to be there, especially if you'd always been at the BBC. It was Greg Dyke, it was post-Burt oppression some might say. I became Controller of BBC Children's. It was a wonderful opportunity, and it was at a critical time when the BBC was planning its future in the multi-channel business. There were lots of discussions and there had already been a lot of early work done on the channels by people like Greg Childs. In fact, BBC kids' existed on one of the multi-channels, so there was already a sort of trial there, but it was one channel – that covered the whole of Children's. We went on to determine we would cover kids from 0 to 13. (Although of course, the Broadcasters Audience Research Board (BARB) still describes kids as 2 to 15, so there's a missing group, and I would say that's the same today.)

There was much discussion about how we could serve kids in a way that was central to the BBC, of being culturally relevant, of being a public service broadcaster and still wanting to be very competitive. There was this interesting dichotomy for public service broadcasters – ratings balanced with the public good. At this time BBC Children's had been dominant, even with the growth of Disney and Nickelodeon – and CITV having enjoyed a more successful time – but BBC Children's was very much the main player.

So the task of the team, and this was a big team – there were three or four hundred people in East Tower [at BBC Television Centre] – was around developing a service for kids that could [actually] reach kids and, remember, at that time only 50% of homes had access to multi-channel, [or] had access to computers. You still had to very much keep your public service core, and we maintained our kids programmes on BBC One and BBC Two, but we looked at what to do to extend our range of programmes, and compete, in those multi-channel environments.

It was a very enhanced budget. The budget when we launched was around £110 million – so the ambition that was set within, by Alan Yentob, Greg Dyke, by the BBC itself, was massive – and was a huge contributory factor to what the team were able to achieve. We had to get permission from the Department for Culture, Media and Sport (DCMS). The process was lengthy and detailed, and this was my introduction to the BBC systems and bureaucracy. I was very much an outsider in that sense, but with a team like Greg Childs, Dot Prior, and some great executives that were central to BBC kids at the time, we developed a proposal that was persuasive about what we wanted to do – and from the outset the team's view was that if you tried to serve all kids from 0 to 13 in one service, you weren't really doing anything that was appropriate, or meeting your goals of serving the British kids audience.

> You don't have to be an expert to realise there's a very big difference between a 4 year old and a 13 year old – and how do you serve them at once? That was one of the challenges for all the linear broadcasters at the time – you have this huge gap.

So we made an argument, and did a lot of work, on proving that with the judicious use of a fantastic library, a heritage that was brilliant, and smart use of episodic commissioning we could service two channels.

The DCMS application was a nine- or ten-month process. I remember going to my first meetings and being tongue-tied (for years ratings had been my benchmark!), having to describe the philosophy of public service broadcasting to huge teams of external people, opinion formers, journalists. (Greg Childs was my brilliant prop in all this.) I understood the core values, but it was how you articulated that to opinion formers and sceptics – and there were lots of sceptics. When I first got the job, I had a phone call from a very senior BBC executive who congratulated me on joining, but made it very clear he did not support two channels – which gave me a timely reminder of the challenge we faced; even within the BBC there were voices saying that was not the way to go.

Through that development, not only did we have to make a case for two channels, both from a political point of view and financially, but we had to sustain quality. You didn't want to paper this too thinly. These shows had to meet certain requirements, and I think that's a credit to the in-house team, but also to the independent producers that we worked with, that we didn't let that quality drop at all.

This of course was against a backdrop of huge criticism and aggressive politics from our competitors in the marketplace. And understandably, as one of the big heavyweights of children's television was now going to mushroom out into the multi-channel world, with all the benefits of having a linear service that could promote it. But I think in the end this story's only good, because we won it, we got approval for the channels.

I can remember it was at the *Royal Television Society Convention* Cambridge that it was announced – and I was with Alan Yentob at the time. Then it was a very fast rundown. We only had something like 5–6 months to launch the channels. I remember there being a fantastic sense that the team has done a brilliant job on achieving this – and now we have this helter-skelter journey to launch. Of course this had an impact on so many more people than just us within the BBC. It affected writers, artists and producers and so many others within the independent sector.

Some of the vision was very top line; that we simply had to serve these two very clearly defined audiences. The [CBeebies] preschool audience wasn't just about the children, it was about carers, it was about parents. We wanted to be a service that had educational elements to it, with soft learning. And we definitely wanted to have not only parental approval, but appeal. It was something that they could join together or something they could feel safe about leaving the children in front of.

A key format element of CBeebies that we developed was 'live presentation'. This was not just title-to-end title, or just a promotions channel – there was a sense of engaging with the audience. All credit to the team there with Paul Smith, we basically created a four-hour clock for the schedule. I wanted a new show to start at the top of every hour. So at *o'clock*, one of the simplest things for a young audience to start learning is that when the big hand is at the top, a new show starts – and it was just a simple bit of time keeping. This, by the way, caused some huge problems with different running times! We worked on a four-hour wheel – if *Teletubbies* was at 1 o'clock it was going to be on at 5 o'clock, and so on. The day was divided into blocks, so every presentation link was different to the one that was in the o'clock before it, and they all had themes. That allowed us to give the sense of the daily schedule being very different all the time, although it often had many of the same elements and the same shows. And I think that very much played to all the objectives we'd had of something fresh, something that was relevant, something that felt inspirational and something that felt new. But at the same time managing it within all the constraints of budgets and timing. The programmes were really strong – we knew we had a great heritage of good programming – and the new commissions were very good, but the live presentation and style of it was the real point of difference of CBeebies.

CBBC was an entirely different issue, and I think continues to be an issue for all channels that are dealing with the 7+ audience. And we didn't have the challenges then that the channels have now. It was far more difficult to give CBBC a cohesive single look. It was much broader, in factual entertainment, entertainment, news and drama. With such a big mix of genres – how did you get an overall brand that appeals to everybody from a 6-year old to 13-year old? In an ideal world we needed a third channel! That would have been perfect. And then you segment that audience, and you'd have crossover, and eventually end up with a young teen audience. Of course, that wasn't to be.

Without a doubt, CBeebies came out of the blocks really quickly; CBBC was a slower build and was known more for its individual programs, rather than its generic whole. I think that's probably something to a certain extent you have to live with – accept that you will have shows that stand out, and that even though all the shows would be good, CBBC didn't have the same resonance with the audience that CBeebies had. They were two different challenges; one I think we did well with, one I think we did OK.

From the outset we wanted 90% British content on CBeebies and 75% on CBBC. And the reason for the difference is CBBC could have an international flavour. It should be able to seek the best of other channels or other producers from around the world. For CBeebies it was more important to be culturally spot on for the audience and reflect the audience both in its diversity and its range. So for us it was of key importance that we stuck to that 90%. What's interesting is there was a strong sense from the competitors about how unfair this was.

I can remember that on the first day that we launched, the DCMS called us – it was Tessa Jowell at the time – to say they had had strong complaints about how many cartoons were on CBBC. We of course had to explain there weren't. But the word cartoon summed up a cultural difference – there was an assumption that these 'cartoons' must all be American. We never called them cartoons. Not because we were being smart, but there was a difference. This became quite an emergency at the time. There were lots of people going "oh my god, you've launched these channels and you've already broken the rules. You've only been on air for four hours!" We had to immediately give a written response to the DCMS, led by Dot Prior. We explained the difference between a cartoon and our animated series, which would have been pre-bought or commissioned by us and largely produced in the UK; that we're not running *Bugs Bunny* back-to-back. But that in a way illustrates some of the cultural interpretations of what we were doing. Every animation that we ran on CBeebies we dubbed into British voices. So we did run some American shows – like *Clifford the Big Red Dog* – which was re-voiced. If there was a show that we really liked that we felt met the values creatively and editorially of the channels, we've revoiced them, so that there was a sense of being relevant to our audience and, of course, we were competing with American channels, who didn't do that, so that was a point of difference. We weren't necessarily complaining about them. This wasn't making any negative comments about them. It was just saying that's our difference. That's what we do. And you know the voices you hear will be British voices reflecting our audience.

I think we should be really proud of the channels, there's no doubt about that. CBeebies in particular was well developed by the team and has grown really well and has lasted. It's very

Photo: by Robert Lamb, CC BY-SA 2.0, https://commons.wikimedia.org/w/index.php?curid=11059994

Photo: Sharron on Flickr

interesting that those little yellow branding amoebas, that they were almost exactly the same at launch as you see them today. CBeebies definitely achieved what we wanted, and has gone on to exceed that.

I was also very proud of what we did with CBBC, but it was a different challenge. It was much harder but there's some great shows that came out of it. But probably, if I look back, we were too dependent on some shows like *Blue Peter* – which I put to five days a week. It was probably the right thing to do for a while to launch the channel but *Blue Peter* is a treasured brand that you can't just spread everywhere. And so I think that was probably an error.

We created a big show called *Xchange*, which was a massive team effort, but did we put too much into too few things? We did some great Drama at times. But again, I find myself even now talking about programmes and not the brand, not the 'overall' – whereas CBeebies I don't talk about the programmes, I talk about the brand, and I think that is a great legacy.

It's just a joy to me that CBeebies is still going strong and it's really good. I love the way it's still talked about and it's still very much part of people's lives. But interestingly, if I look at my four grandchildren, they're only interested in shows. They know CBeebies, but they're not watching on TV, they're watching on tablets and phones; their watching is very different. If we were planning today, god knows how we would do it!

KiKA at 25: Constant Change, Constant Challenges

Sebastian Debertin, Head of International Content Acquisitions & Co-Productions, KiKA

KiKA is a free-to-air German public service broadcasting television children's channel, set up jointly by ARD and ZDF.

This year KiKA is celebrating its 25th anniversary and, looking back, I'm reminded of the constant changes and challenges the channel has faced over those years – and no doubt, will do so in the future. Please forgive me for perhaps stating the obvious, but we are living through interesting and more than difficult times.

Today, the situation is not easy for us adults, but it is even more problematic for our kids, both in the UK and here on the continent. These challenges are unprecedented. A year ago I couldn't imagine it could get any worse when I mused: "Oh, my poor children and their poor friends and classmates, all the restrictions and difficulties in times of Covid and the huge threat of climate change – what a mess!" What a splendid and golden childhood my generation had enjoyed compared to them. Yes, we had no internet, no smartphones, but we played outside (fantastic!), building treehouses or silly dams in the little stream nearby, built campfires and told wild and totally weird stories or we were doing other useless stuff that nevertheless taught us on many levels so much. Well, as we say here in Thuringia, memory always writes in golden letters.

We did, however, not have to face a pandemic, nor did we face the constant distraction of social media that demands our ears' and eyeballs' attention. Nowadays kids are also being forced to fight for the environmental future of this planet. And on top of that, they have to see us adults struggling to handle a war at our neighbour's garden fence. That brings up new, even more frightening fears for the future of the younger generation. Oh, I sound too dark now, right? I apologise! And yes, a few months ago, I would have sounded more positive. "Ha! In Covid times, more positive. Why?" Well, because I saw kids' resilience growing. I personally found it very encouraging to learn that many kids were adapting much better to the Covid-restrictions in their lives than some of us adults. I saw them making the best of the situation they found themselves in, keeping contact with friends through their smartphones – while their classes had been torn apart – and doing home schooling more or less successfully. They read more books than ever and, lucky us, they were not too

Image: © KiKA

engrossed in *Minecraft*, *Roblox* and co., like some others might have been. (By the way, regarding *Roblox* and co: no, I don't think public service broadcasters need to be in this area, or in the Metaverse, even though the kids are. But we do have to ensure, first and foremost, that we join the discussion to make these new worlds safe for children!)

Back in 2020, like all Public Service Broadcasters (PSBs) worldwide, KiKA was challenged by Covid and quickly had to adapt large parts of our programming in order to meet the altered and new needs of our various kids' audiences – with children of all ages constantly at home, being home-schooled for many, many months. Yes, my children, being home-schooled by me – what a horror for my kids! I finally learned that it was the right decision not to become a teacher... Bless all the wonderful people who take up this challenging job! Thank you, dear teachers of the world!

At KiKA we created appropriate campaigns for the Covid-times, letting kids know that "we are standing together in this crisis," like the 'Gemeinsam Zuhause' (home together) campaign (with supporting materials for children's crafts, recipes, etc). We did indeed all have to stand together at home. We were doing our jobs, while taking care of our kids' homeschooling, their education, alongside the usual daily frenzy and joy of bringing up kids.

Image: © KiKA

For some kids, especially in lower-income families, there will be no golden memories of the Covid-time. Many of the disadvantaged were suffering disproportionately. So it was good to see that a number of kids started to engage more strongly than ever in the fight for children's rights! In April 2022, I was happy to listen to 12 year old Ella from Hamburg (member of the KiKA Award Jury) become the first child ever to present on ARD's Tagesthemen (nationwide late evening news). Ella commented on the war in Ukraine, in relation to the United Nations' Convention on the Rights of Children, and directly demanded of the German chancellor "Mr. Scholz, to include children's rights in the German Grundgesetz" (the German constitution). Bravo, Ella! That is a challenge worth fighting for!

Another challenge, and truly worth the fight, is advocating for the future of PSBs, worldwide. I must say I follow the licence fee discussions in the UK with great concern. Although it is obviously difficult to judge developments in the UK, it seems to me that the situation for PSB is more problematic in the UK than for PSBs here in Germany. Clearly in Germany we need to find answers to various tricky questions, like how to renew the PSBs for tomorrow's needs and challenges. We also constantly need to find answers to whether certain politicians are right that PSBs should only concentrate on education and news coverage. Well, I tend to simply answer as follows: the 'Rundfunkbeitrag', the broadcasting fee, as it is called here in Germany, is meant to fund Deutschlandradio, ARD and ZDF including KiKA, and is in place to secure access to a *full* media service for *all* people in Germany. The fee is paid by every household and ensures that everybody can participate in our society, even low-income households, who can apply successfully for a fee rebate.

Regardless of some politicians from time-to-time calling for a narrower focus, I am convinced that PSBs, not only in Germany, but worldwide, also need popular entertainment and, yes, even Hollywood fare, to attract viewers' interest. PSB services with a narrow news and culture focus would be in a dead-end, serving a small niche. I am sure their future would soon be brought into question by the same politicians. Not allowing PSBs to offer popular genres is – from my personal point of view – just arguing for the sake of commercial rivals, and would be unfair to both the audience and to the quality of output provided by the PSBs! We need to better communicate that PSBs, across the globe, are a strong pillar of our democratic societies, now and in the future.

The media landscape has evolved a lot in the 25 years of KiKA's existence, creating challenge after challenge for PSBs. A recent example is a consequence of the 'Medienstaatsvertrag' state treaty, which came into effect from November 2020 and regulates the obligations and rights of media providers in Germany. The treaty heavily limits acquisition of non-European programs by PSBs; for example, they are only allowed to be broadcast on linear services. However, with the commercial rivals free to do what they want, the audience can't understand this restriction. Parents and their kids are complaining intensively: "We do not care where the programs come from, we care for good programs and we pay our licence fee (for the programs), so we want to have access to all KiKA-programs, linear and non-linear, any time, at home or on the go!" To my mind, they are right.

Where is the sense in such limitation of PSBs *only* – when both commercial and PSB providers are mastering, more or less, the huge job of transformation into a multi-platform digital future? It is like putting ankle-cuffs around Germany's PSBs' legs at the start of the digital marathon race. It's unfair, right? For the sake of diverse and various audiences, we need fair competition. Our mission is simply to provide all people, today and in the future, independently from their income, with information, education, advice and yes, also entertainment – no matter whether the programs come from Germany, from Europe or from all over the world! We need to continue to work on building a fair media landscape in which PSBs should play a significant part, now and in the future.

It is also more important than ever that we collaborate with other pubcasters to fulfil this mission. For many years now, we have been working with partners assembled via the EBU (European Broadcasting Union), with a good collaboration success story being the *Junior Eurovision Song Contest*. Co-productions are a tremendously important tool in times of shrinking budgets, especially when licence fee decreases are in discussion and money, for some, is additionally going from programming budgets into digital-distribution and -transmission costs. These co-pros offer a cornucopia of advantages – bringing added value and quality in terms of content, team, production, diversity and especially highest production value. A recent and very successful example being the co-pro animated series *Dog Loves Books* which we at KiKA, alongwith beside many others, enjoyed co-producing with colleagues at the BBC. *Dog Loves Books* was produced by Komixx Entertainment (now renamed to iGeneration studios) and is a truly wonderful show, designed to remind children that there are fantastic things, and even broader worlds, to discover when reading a book!

It's 25 years since the decision was made by ARD and ZDF to join forces and build a kids' channel – initially named Der Kinderkanal, and now contracted to KiKA. Not everybody in the Germany of 1997 truly welcomed a public TV service dedicated to kids, especially not the commercial competition. But strong people fought for the

Image: © KiKA

project, for the sake of the kids' audience. I remember very well Theresa Plummer-Andrews, who at that time, along with others at the BBC, were similarly fighting for kids' PSB in the UK. Plummer-Andrews was part of a BBC delegation that came visiting KiKA in the build up to the launch of CBBC and CBeebies. Her opening comment at our debriefing session was clear, straightforward and relevant as always: "Well, dear German fellows, we won't make the mistake you made! We will fight for more than one channel in order to give appropriate service to the pre-schoolers, the 6–9-kids and 10+ audience!" Theresa Plummer-Andrews, who later was more known to me as 'Plumtrees', and her strong colleagues at the BBC were absolutely right, and so they accepted the challenge. They did successfully fight for what they found important, for the sake of the children in the UK!

Well, as already stated, we are living in interesting and constantly challenging times. I am confident and hopeful however that the next generation will stand up and accept the new and upcoming challenges. And I am sure that in the end the arguments which we in Germany, as well as in the UK, have for kids' PSB services, are the stronger ones, and will continue to be worth the fight, for the sake of our children!

It Isn't Easy Being Green for Fifty Years: Sesame Street's UK Anniversary

David Kleeman, SVP Global Trends, Dubit Ltd

This article is adapted from '"Street Gang" Tells Us How We Got To "Sesame Street"', published by the Children's Media Foundation in January 2022.

In 1971, *Sesame Street* came to UK television screens for the first time. From controversial beginnings, it has become one of the longest running children's shows, loved by generation after generation.

Created a few years earlier, *Sesame Street* was revolutionary in the US, taking a whole new approach to children's content and debuting a year before the founding of Public Service Broadcasting (PBS). It had a controversial start in the UK, with debate on whether or not to broadcast the show lasting two years. The BBC emphatically rejected *Sesame Street* as too middle-class. However ITV cautiously picked it up for trials (on HTV) and it soon became a staple in the children's schedule.

Today, children's media tend to cater to tightly-focused target ages closely attuned to developmental hallmarks. It has highly-specific content, themes or curriculum; an explicit 'need' to be fulfilled; and distribution and marketing patterns honed to promote discovery and engagement. *Sesame Street*, by contrast, is aimed at developing the whole child, weaving together cognitive, social, emotional and cultural objectives.

Sesame Street's pioneering experiments have provided invaluable research, insights and techniques that children's media (not just TV) creators bring to bear in our work daily. Child development hasn't changed in 50 years. What varies widely over time and across cultures is the context in which kids grow and learn. *Sesame*

Photo (modifications made): Frosted with Emotion on Flickr

Street has always honored the timeless hallmarks of every child's development. With this as a firm base, the series has been free to incorporate timely or sensitive content.

In its early days, Muppet 'Roosevelt Franklin' was an explicitly Black character, as the series sought to engage children who'd seldom known a TV character who looked or talked like them. The global history of *Sesame Street* is similarly replete with daring examples. 'Kami', who is HIV+, is a character in the South African *Sesame Street* co-production; there was also an Israeli-Palestinian co-production; and a metaphoric episode on 'fear' shortly after 9/11. More recently, *Sesame Street* has popped up as a political stalking horse – should 'Big Bird' have gotten a COVID vaccination?

These are difficult topics to address and present for children, but *Sesame Street* has always met these ideas head-on. Series composer Joe Raposo captured the series ethos in discussing the song *It isn't easy being green*: "We're not sure what we are or what we can be; we know there's potential and the realization to accept ourselves. To know that we can become something perhaps we never dreamed we could be. That's what *Sesame Street* is about."

More than fifty years on, *Sesame Street* is still helping children around the world figure out how to be their version of green.

Boom Plant
Cynhyrchwyr cynnwys llinol a digidol aml-genre
i blant 0 – 13 mlwydd oed.

Boom Kids
Award winning producers of linear and digital, multi-genre
content for children 0 – 13 years old.

Ten Years Keeping On Keeping On

Jayne Kirkham, Public Contact and Clerk for the All-Party Parliamentary Group (APPG) for Children's Arts and Media

There was a time when the world of children's media in the UK seemed a simple and lovely, rosy place: there were a handful of TV channels each producing their fair share of programmes across all genres and formats for all ages up to and including 16. Commissioners commissioned, producers produced: everyone went about their business, perhaps not quite in a state of bliss, but certainly with a sense of certainty about the future.

Then in 2003, the Government's Communications Bill became law. Like the moment when the Titanic bumped into the iceberg, there was little reaction at first. But by 2010, the full impact was being felt: as the only public service broadcaster with any real budget, the BBC was all powerful, the international broadcasters (there were now at least 35 digital channels for kids) wanted more international content, or cheap repeats or both and unable to compete, our homegrown production companies and studios were closing. Ofcom reported that of all the content available to children, only 1% was new and made in the UK. The rich varied diet of linear TV had gone and children were binge-watching endless hours of repeats and imports. And something had to be done.

Since the closure of Granada Kids in 2006, the forerunner of the Children's Media Foundation Save Kids TV had recognised that as it was an act of parliament that had done all this damage, so it would need parliament to act to put things right. But nobody in parliament was particularly interested. Individual MPs thought children should be running around outside anyway and the gatekeepers at the Department for Culture, Media and Sport (DCMS) kept the gates firmly shut. We did get to go to some rather nice parliamentary receptions though. It was at one of these that I managed to bypass the aides and advisors and actually speak with the then Secretary of State for DCMS, Ben Bradshaw. "You should start an APPG," he said. "Really?" I replied. "Yes, go and do it."

That was early 2010 and the idea seemed impossible. But two things happened: Floella Benjamin was ennobled, joining the House of Lords as a Liberal Democrat, and the 2010 General Election returned a hung parliament with the Conservative party forming a coalition with the… Liberal Democrats.

We finally had a voice in Westminster and the connections I had made at those rather nice parliamentary receptions began to pay off. Tom Watson, Lisa Nandy, Graham Stuart, Damian Hinds, Ed Vaizey, Lord Clement-Jones, Baroness Massey, to name a few, all lent their support and we soon had enough people across all parties and houses to start a group that would support and champion not just children's media but their arts as well. It was pretty clear to all of us that children don't overly differentiate between 'art' and 'entertainment' or 'education' and 'play' and so neither should we. This APPG would join the dots between all the forms of creativity offered to children and between the governmental departments that should be serving them.

This meant that the APPG has had a huge remit, ranging from traditional TV to specialist theatre, from online safety to music in the school curriculum... in-app purchasing, turning STEM into STEAM, child performers...

But All-Party Parliamentary Groups are not select committees: they have no power within parliament. What they can have is influence. They are an opportunity for interested parties to meet with interested parliamentarians. So over the years, we have invited those who know and care to share their expertise, raising the awareness of parliamentarians who do have the power. For example:

- Reg Bailey considered whether the recommendations in his government-sponsored independent review into the commercialisation and sexualisation of childhood had been actioned.
- Ian Douthwaite used his research at Dubit to bust myths about what children are really doing online and give politicians a reality check.
- Oli Hyatt and Greg Chapman from Animation UK brought a collection of well-loved animation characters that added momentum to the campaign for the animation tax break.
- Vicky Ireland and David Wood from Action For Children's Arts highlighted the inequalities of public funding for children's arts and called on the UK to live up to its responsibilities as a signatory to the UN Rights of the Child.
- David Austin from the BBFC demonstrated how easily children could access online pornography in the debate over age-verification.
- Katy Jones arranged for over 100 parliamentarians to receive a copy of the BBC's *Ten Pieces* video, raising their awareness of the importance of music education in children's lives and society as a whole.
- Professor Jeanette Steemers shared the results of her investigation into contestable funding in other countries.
- Baroness Kidron screened her documentary *InRealLife* raising awareness of the effects of the internet on young people.

Plus more besides, contributing to debates and parliamentary business with verbal and written questions asked in both houses. Given how busy Westminster is, and given how many other areas of life have a greater priority, it has always been a struggle to get the attention we believe these issues deserve. But despite elections, referenda, parliamentary crises, ministers hired and fired, departmental changes and the rules and procedures that these throw at APPGs, the group has punched above its weight. It has played a part in:

- Successfully curbing in-app purchases in children's online games, alongside the Office of Fair Trading.

- Securing an amendment to the Children's and Families Bill regarding children's performance licence agreements.
- Action For Children's Arts' on-going *Cultural Backpack* pilot which aims to provide all primary school children with five cultural experiences in the school year.
- Successfully amending the Digital Economy Bill to give Ofcom the power to urge commercial public service broadcasters to commission more children's content.
- Successfully amending the Digital Economy Bill to introduce age verification to commercial online pornography sites.
- Securing the animation tax break, and then securing it to take in all children's content.
- Securing £57m of the Government's proposed £60m contestable fund for Children's public service content in its three-year pilot.

There is still much to do. Whereas we should still have been riding high on the achievements of the past ten years, February brought us down to earth with a bump with the news that the Young Audiences Content Fund was closing. Perhaps we all should have known – it was a three-year pilot after all and the three years were nearly up. But all the news we were getting was of its success and there was nothing to suggest it wouldn't continue. (Although, actually, there was. But it was buried so deep in the bowels of Whitehall that it was only after the fact that anybody found anything that might have served as a warning.) So, the first half of this year has been spent garnering support and amassing evidence to take to the latest Secretary of State. She has made it clear that the Fund won't be reinstated, so we are making it clear that the Industry it breathed life back into, is now in a worse place than ever with the only viable public service commissioner, the BBC, cutting its children's content by the back-door, and the commercial PSBs under greater threat from the big international companies online. And add to that, the post-pandemic, post-Brexit financial position the country finds itself in – children's arts and media are going to get pushed way down the list of priorities if we're not careful.

Photo: by Tanaphong Toochinda on Unsplash

But children should be our priority, they are our future. As Baroness Benjamin says, "Childhood lasts a lifetime." We all know that arts and media made especially for children nurtures and nourishes them, helping them make sense of themselves and the world they are born into. The APPG will be going back to basics and making sure the people whose policies affect them know, understand and ensure that a healthy, vibrant and resilient children's creative industry helps raise healthy, vibrant and resilient children – now and as adults of the future. We just have to keep on keeping on.

A Beginner's Guide to Herding Cats: Or How to Coordinate a Campaign on the Future of Public Service Media for Children

Colin Ward, Deputy Director, Children's Media Foundation

The Children's Media Foundation (CMF) exists to encourage the creation of rich, varied media experiences for children that helps them to understand the world they live in, to discover new things to do and see and to ask questions that will support their growth and development. But I've discovered that the CMF is also a dedicated group of ninja cat herders.

Or at least that is how it felt for most of 2021 and into 2022, as we launched the CMF's report on the future of public service media for children – *Our children's future: does public service media matter?* – and continued our engagement with government and the children's production community to further those goals. The report discussed everything from the teen audience for Netflix's *Bridgerton* to the unique and offbeat qualities you find in some of the best storytelling conceived and written for the UK children's audience. Our writers offered comprehensive, well-researched overviews on policy, production and public service in the UK. They tackled inclusivity, alternative funding streams for public service media, the impact of new technologies and changes to children's media preferences and – of particular relevance over the last two years – the important role children's public service media can play in government health campaigns.

All that hard work laid the foundations for the CMF's public service media campaign, which has continued into 2022 with events, letters and petitions, meetings with Ofcom and the Department for Culture, Media and Sport (DCMS) and further research. And as part of that campaign, we have done our best to keep all interested parties involved in the work and – more or less – pulling in the same direction. That is where the cat herding comes into play.

The CMF knows that, as a society, we can only meet the needs of the children's audience if we have a thriving children's media

production sector. So we are often engaged in persuading both government and the production industry on the importance of aligning their policies to the needs of the audience, because although everyone is in broad agreement on the aims of the campaign, there is never complete agreement on how to define the problem or on what needs to be done to remedy the situation.

Understandably, every group responds to a broad church campaign with an eye on its own agenda, whether that is a politician intent on exploring alternative mechanisms for funding public service media, a publisher or broadcaster keen to defend their own platform, or a trade body that needs to defend the interests of its members. So there have been moments when the CMF has relaxed a little, thinking we have managed to get one of the cats heading in a helpful direction, only to be told, from out of nowhere, that the government has decided its BBC agenda requires an arbitrary and destructive decision to axe the Young Audiences Content Fund (YACF), going against everything they had been saying in public in the run up to the announcement. And then, while you are frantically trying to get that particular cat back in line, someone else decides the solution to children's media funding has to be better tax breaks, because that is "something government will at least consider."

The CMF is always sympathetic to these different priorities and we understand why some of these decisions have been taken. As an example, better tax breaks are clearly helpful and are often a good option for encouraging sector growth, particularly if you are a producer developing co-production projects that are attractive to international partners. But they are perhaps less helpful if you want to make live-action, UK-cultural content because, with the demise of the YACF, there is not enough money on offer to get those ideas developed and commissioned in the first place – so the offer of a tax break to *potential* funders is cold comfort. Previously a live-action producer might have turned to the BBC, but BBC Children's has other challenges to face and is currently falling head-over-heels in love with animation, partly to satisfy Ofcom's agenda, which is to make sure the BBC's children's services grow their audience. So for a live-action producer that funding option is now looking like a steep cliff to climb. When you look at the whole picture and consider the needs of the audience, improved tax breaks can only ever be part of the solution.

It is the role of the CMF to consider that larger picture. We are working hard to keep the different groups talking and listening to each other, so we can agree on a way forward that works for everyone: a proposal that meets the needs of big and small producers working in both live-action and animation; that the children's media community, speaking with one voice, can put to government; a new funding model that protects the BBC's relationship with the audience at this critical moment in its history, but also allows commercial public service media platforms to access additional public money to address the market failure in UK-originated content for children identified by both PACT and Ofcom; and, the most important consideration from the CMF perspective, a proposal that acknowledges children's media experiences are about much more than 'channel watching' and that is capable of delivering a rich and varied diet of media content, including UK-originated content, across all genres. How do we create a robust public service media structure that provides children with the content they want to see that is also available on the platforms they want to use?

The one group that always seems to be heading in the same direction as the CMF is the creative people who make children's content; the producers, directors, writers, editors, performers and all the talented craft professionals who are working on UK-originated children's content that, despite all the obstacles, is still getting made. In 2021, they contributed articles to the CMF's report on public service media for children, they helped fund the CMF's work and they rallied behind our campaigns, signing petitions and sharing our ideas to raise awareness of the debate. We know that the majority of people working in children's media production are motivated by a desire to tell stories to a diverse children's audience and we recognise that they simply can't do that work unless it is properly funded. We are hugely grateful for their support.

The Children's Media Foundation will not stop. We will continue to build alliances and lobby the government. We remain determined to change the nature of this debate, putting the needs of the audience at the top of the agenda and avoiding short-term, politically-motivated decision making. If you would like to play an active role in our campaign work then please get in touch.

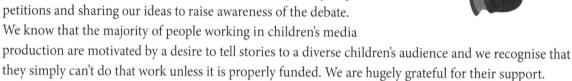

THE CHILDREN'S MEDIA FOUNDATION THANKS

nickelodeon™

FOR THEIR SUPPORT FOR THE YEARBOOK 2022

The Children's Media Foundation thanks

milkshake!
Sunshine every day from 6am

for their support for The Children's Media Yearbook 2022

www.milkshake.tv Instagram: @milkshake_tv
Youtube.com/milkshaken5 FB.com/MilkshakeTVUK

milkshake! 5

Continuing Failures on Policy Around Children's Screen Content – the Demise of the **Young Audiences Content Fund** and the BBC's Strategy for Children's Content

Prof Jeanette Steemers, Professor of Culture, Media & Creative Industries, King's College London

In January this year on the British Film Institute's website, it was quietly announced that the UK government's Department for Digital, Culture, Media & Sport (DDCMS) would be ending the three year pilot for the Young Audiences Content Fund (YACF) and that applications for funding and developing children's content would close on 25th February. Since it began in 2019 with £57m over three years sourced from leftover licence fee funding from digital rollout, the fund has supported 144 development projects and 55 new productions, commissioned by the commercial Public Service Broadcasters (PSBs) (ITV, Five, Channel Four) and language broadcasters S4C and BBC Alba. These have included *The World According to Grandpa* (Five /S4C), *Makeaway Takeaway* (CITV), *How* (CiTV), *Teen First Dates* (E4), *Letters in Lockdown* (E4/All4), *Quentin Blake's Clown* (C4), *FYI News Specials* (Sky News and First News), *Mimi's World* (Five) and many more still in production. The public service credentials of the fund are incontrovertible, fulfilling criteria on quality, innovation, additionality, nations and regions, diversity, new voices, plurality and reach.

The YACF, under Director Jackie Edwards, represented a joined up intervention from the UK's communications regulator, Ofcom, and the government in response to years of market failure in the provision of UK-originated children's screen content, where commercial public service broadcasters no longer felt it was economically viable to support children's commissions. Before the YACF, commissioning of children's PSB content had become largely the preserve of the BBC, whose own funds are under pressure. Closing the fund reverts the sector back to 2019, when the BBC was practically the only commissioning PSB.

The government's decision is disappointing given its recent (June 2021) commitment to YACF in its response to the House of Commons Digital, Culture, Media and Sport Select Committee's inquiry into the Future of Public Service Broadcasting[1]. The committee recommended that the Government evaluate YACF's success against its goals and extend the scheme "if it is found to be increasing the investment in original content for children in the UK." The DDCMS duly complied, agreeing that "children's programming is an essential source of entertainment and learning for young people in the UK" and that it was "committed to ensuring young audiences have access to engaging and relevant content that reflects UK society and their own diverse experiences across the nations and regions." In its response the government said it would undertake a full pilot evaluation to determine impact "on the provision and plurality of public service content for young audiences" and that a decision on the future of the fund (closure, maintenance or expansion) would only take place after "detailed evaluation of the scheme." This regrettably has not happened.

What did happen between June 2021 and January 2022 was the Secretary of State's decision about the future of the licence fee. In her letter to the BBC on 21 January[2] the Secretary of State said there would be no deduction through "contestable funding." This may have signalled the end for the YACF, as the DDCMS did not specify any alternative funding sources for the fund, and the announcement of its closure followed shortly afterwards – in contrast to recent DDCMS awards to the gaming sector (£8m) and the UK Global Screen Fund (£21m).

The Children's Media Foundation coordinated a response from various groups and individuals, asking the Secretary of State to reconsider and grant the YACF an extension and direct DDCMS funding of £10m a year – at least until there is a clearer sense of a wider BBC review. Without the YACF, which provided up to 50% of production budgets, the commercial PSBs may simply stop supporting UK children's content – and the Ofcom strategy for children's commercial public service content involving encouragement of commercial PSBs would fall apart. Changes at BBC Children's with closer alignment to BBC Studios and more investment in animation also suggest that children's drama and factual programming will be affected (see below).

Pressures on children's content production are complicated by the BBC's announcement on 27th May (as we went to press) that the CBBC channel may close within the next 3–6 years in favour of a digital first proposition on the iPlayer. A more concerted digital strategy is welcome, but the move raises serious questions about universal free access for all audiences and the danger of a greater 'digital divide', if growing numbers of children and families can't afford broadband, and therefore access to BBC services, alongside heating and food.

The CBBC announcement arrived hard on the heels of Ofcom's decision, also in May 2022, following consultation to change the operating licence of the CBBC channel, to allow a reduction in original production transmission (including repeats, but excluding acquisitions) from 72% to 66% from 2022–23, and up to 68% in 2024 (with

---

[1] https://www.gov.uk/government/publications/bbc-and-s4c-final-2022-licence-fee-settlement-letters/letter-from-secretary-of-state-to-bbc-on-final-determination-of-the-2022-licence-fee-settlement

[2] https://www.gov.uk/government/publications/bbc-and-s4c-final-2022-licence-fee-settlement-letters/letter-from-secretary-of-state-to-bbc-on-final-determination-of-the-2022-licence-fee-settlement

this following an Ofcom approved reduction in 2019 of CBBC originations from 400 to 350 hours, and of *Newsround* hours from 85 to 35 hours a year). This all suggests that Children's is not at the forefront of the BBC's pressing priorities, and ironically with the relaunch of BBC3 as a linear channel in January 2022, CBBC's transmission hours were cut by 2 hours a day – back to 7pm.

The changes the BBC are allowed to make now need to be considered in the light of its renewed dominance as a public service commissioner of UK children's content, following the closure of the YACF. What also needs to be considered are the implications for the nations and regions (Scotland, Wales and Northern Ireland), particularly if an increase in animation over time results in fewer regional voices. The extra savings will be invested in three new animation series a year (up to 32 hours a year) to shore up audiences on CBBC, but with little revealed about how these will be "rooted in British culture" in a production environment driven by international considerations, and probably at the expense of live action drama and factual content. There is nothing wrong with wanting to make more animation, particularly if these are distinctive, of the highest quality and reflect the UK's diverse communities (BBC Public Purpose 3 and 4). However, the case for animation at the expense of drama, for example, is not clearly made, particularly in relation to funding. Assumptions about a majority of children between the ages of 5–7 (70%) watching animation on video-sharing platforms (2.13) seem overstated. It does not refer to 8–12 year olds, the older section of CBBC's target audience, and does not reflect Ofcom's own findings in its latest Media Use and Attitudes

Report (March 2022)[3] that suggest the most watched content on video sharing platforms are 'funny videos' (65% of children aged 3–17; and 60% of 5–7s), alongside a variety of other content including music videos (51%), gaming tutorials (43%), learning videos (41%), how-to videos (39%) and whole programmes (33%) (pp.27–28) – which is reflected in the popularity of short-form videos and influencers (pp. 28- 29).

An increase in animation on the CBBC channel and later online may help to engage audiences, but this is not guaranteed, and underplays children's wider interests (educational, factual, gaming, comedy) that clearly extend beyond animation on rival channels and digital platforms.

> "a significant minority of children aged 8-15 think there is not enough content that reflects where they live (over one third) or shows children that look like them (25%)"

Of course, the largest question mark exists over funding. To what extent will the BBC's financial resources for children (which remain 'broadly the same' as per its submission to Ofcom) be channelled towards animation, for example, and how will budgets be balanced across animation, drama, entertainment and factual – and also reflect crucial regional considerations across production and content. Any changes require careful monitoring, but recent developments suggest the continuing erosion of regulation that protects the provision of children's screen content – both within the BBC and among commercial PSBs. This is concerning when a significant minority of children aged 8–15 think there is not enough content that

---

[3] https://www.ofcom.org.uk/research-and-data/media-literacy-research/childrens

reflects where they live (over one third) or shows children that look like them (25%). Transnational and budgetary pressures are certainly ever present, but the BBC needs to offer something distinctive.

The future of public service children's content is desperately in peril and its funding needs to be openly debated in terms of the developing media landscape, and the possible impacts on children and the trained professionals who cater for this market. The BBC is a vital actor in this sector, and therefore decisions about its funding and resourcing will have profound implications for both young audiences and children's media creators. Any reduction in CBBC output of original productions and increases in animation content to possibly attract larger audiences should not be decided in haste without careful consultation, safeguards and robust evidence, because there are considerable risks over time that BBC content for children will eventually become indistinguishable from other providers – with this chipping away at what a public service operator should be doing for children and society overall. There are no easy answers of course, but the current BBC strategy for its youngest audiences raises serious questions that require nuanced and careful responses.

Prof Jeanette Steemers is Chair of the YACF's advisory Steering Committee and is Chair of the YACF Users Committee. The views expressed here are her own and do not represent the BFI or YACF. This is an extended version of an earlier piece for the Voice of the Listener and Viewer April 2022 Bulletin.

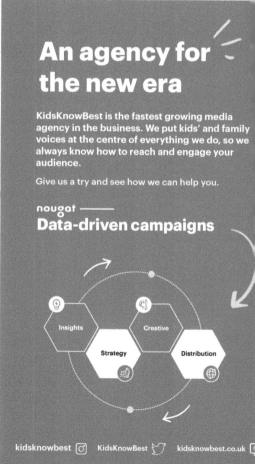

Playful by Design

Prof Sonia Livingstone, Professor of Social Psychology, LSE and **Dr Kruakae Pothong**, Researcher, Digital Futures Commission

Children's play has a rich history and takes near infinite forms. It's vital for their development, learning, self-expression and sense of belonging. It includes but goes broader than activities formally organised as games.

But even in relatively privileged wealthy countries, children are losing opportunities for play. Green spaces have been disappearing. Children are driven instead of walking to school. Free time is sacrificed to the demands of the school curriculum. Parents fear letting children play by themselves. Where play is supported, this is frequently harnessed to serve adult agendas, often commercial, but even when intended to benefit children's learning or health, for example, a consequence is that 'free play' – child-led, imaginative, voluntary, open-ended – is particularly under threat.

As children spend more time playing online, it is imperative to ask whether they can play freely in digital contexts? Most digital products and services where children play – or act playfully – are not designed with their needs and rights in mind; far from it. So, could the digital environment be better designed to enhance and not undermine children's free play? What, practically, can digital providers do differently?

The Digital Futures Commission seeks to answer these questions as part of an applied 'play in a digital world' research project aiming to embed children's rights in the digital world. In relation to play, we start not with computer games or social media but by going back to first principles – the qualities of free play and how to design both physical and digital environments to support them. We're intrigued that, still, most people think about free play as taking place in person, offline. A child playing creatively with a cardboard box puts a smile on parents' faces. Everyone loves to recall their own childhood play outside, with muddy knees and no eye on the clock.

While of course we need more and better access to playgrounds, parks, play streets and green spaces, we don't really know how to identify places for children's free play online. Do they, can they exist? What's the digital equivalent of playing with a cardboard box? Is it *Minecraft*, for instance, and if not, why not?

To answer these research questions, we used a mix of methods including literature reviews, expert interviews, public consultation and survey. Our literature reviews identified the prototypical qualities of child-led play or free play and the factors that shape children's free play possibilities. Our online public consultation focused on children's playful experiences in both digital and non-digital contexts and play from the perspectives of parents, caregivers and professionals working with children. Our survey focused on children's evaluation of the qualities of play they experience and the digital features they encounter.

We heard loud and clear from children through our consultation and survey that children seek similar qualities of play wherever they play. From our survey, more children aged 6 to 17 found that play in the non-digital context was more diverse, stimulating, open-ended, imaginative, emotionally resonant and safe than they did play in the digital context. These children also found greater sense of achievement when playing in a non-digital context than playing with digital devices. That said, more children found that play with digital devices offered social and immersive opportunities than playing in a non-digital context.

What works? From the statistical correlations between the qualities and features children reported in our survey, we begin to see which digital features enhance or constrain free play. We highlight seven design principles here. To claim the label 'Playful by Design', digital products and services should adopt seven key recommendations:

1. **Be welcoming:** Prioritise digital features that are inclusive, sociable and welcoming to all, reducing hateful communication and forms of exclusion and reflecting multiple identities.

2. **Enhance imagination:** Prioritise creative resources and imaginative, open-ended play over pre-determined pathways built on popularity metrics or driven by advertising or other commercial pressures.

3. **Enable open-ended play:** Provide and enhance features that offer easy-to-use pathways, flexibility and variety as these support children's agency and encourage their imaginative, stimulating and open-ended play.

4. **No commercial exploitation:** Reduce compulsive features designed to prolong user engagement or cultivate dependency on games, apps or platforms, so children's immersive play is intrinsically motivated and freely chosen.

5. **Ensure safety:** Ensure children's play in online spaces is safe, including by giving them control over who can contact them and supplying help when needed.

6. **Allow for experimentation:** Recognise that exploration, invention and a degree of risk taking is important in children's play and that the burden should not fall on them always to be cautious or anxious, or to follow rules set by others.

7. **Be age-appropriate:** Respect the needs of children of different ages by providing age-appropriate opportunities for play, while also allowing for safe intergenerational play.

It seems that the more inclusive the digital environment is, the more intrinsic motivation the children have to play. Here, by inclusive, we mean welcoming and tolerant. This correlation also suggests that the voluntary nature of children's play is undermined by compulsive features that make it hard for children to stop playing even when children have had enough. So, designing mechanisms to help children wind down from their play would be sensible.

Providing digital products and services that are more inclusive, affordable, and with more targeted support for children when they encounter things that they find upsetting will also make children feel safer in their play. Last but not least, digital products and services that feature engaging design, but offer safe spaces, can encourage children's risk-taking or boundary-pushing play.

Our project addresses policymakers, designers and developers, for they have the power to ensure that the opportunities available to children respect their rights – to play, but also to expression, assembly, privacy, safety and more. In our interviews with children, we find they are intrigued by our proposal for Playful by Design and some of them have sought us out to ask what a rights-respecting approach would involve. But of course it can be tricky to make the digital environment fair for everyone to play in and that it can be challenging to provide for, for example, boundary-pushing play within safe parameters. So, now we are running workshops with designers to establish some good examples for these difficult balancing acts, and to create a design toolkit to promote Playful by Design in practice.

Photo (imposed on tablet): Image Catalog on Flickr

The Children's Sector Speaking as One Voice on the **Online Safety Bill**

 Izzy Wick, Director of Policy, 5Rights

The Online Safety Bill is a major piece of legislation that has the power to transform the digital world as we know it by establishing a new regulatory framework to tackle online harms. Without some significant changes to the draft Bill, however, the government will not live up to its promises of making the UK the safest place in the world to go online, or to give children the highest levels of protection.

In May, nearly 40 organisations – including 5Rights Foundation, NSPCC, Barnardo's, and the Children's Society – came together to speak as one voice on the issues that are most important for children today and for future generations.

Digital technologies have the potential to inspire children, to inform them and to unleash their creativity. Children must not be locked out of the digital world. Their safety and autonomy online must be protected within it. The Bill should ensure that the tech sector creates services that are safe by design and default and they must be held accountable when they fail to do so.

The children's sector called on the government to take action in five areas:

1. Children's rights

99% of children in the UK went online in 2021[1]. Too often we hear online safety and freedom of expression pitted against each other as diametrically opposite, forgetting that children also have a right to freedom of expression. They must not be locked out of services they are entitled to use or have their voices silenced. An Online Safety Bill that focuses on content moderation and removal will undermine children's rights to express themselves and participate freely and safely in the digital world.

The Bill should be amended so that children's experiences and needs sit at its heart, and their rights to freedom of expression, participation and protection from abuse are upheld.

This can be achieved in three ways. The first is to shift the Bill's focus from addressing harmful content regulation to making services safe by design. This would steer the legislation out of the murky waters of freedom of expression and censorship towards a systems-based approach that

---

[1] Ofcom (2022) Children and parents: media use and attitudes report. [https://www.ofcom.org.uk/__data/assets/pdf_file/0024/234609/childrens-media-use-and-attitudes-report-2022.pdf].

focuses less on content moderation and removal and more on the design features and functionalities that account for the spread and scale of harm.

The second is to establish a statutory user advocacy model funded by the industry levy that provides expertise on children's issues. Such a body would ensure the new regime is informed by children's experiences and provides vital counterbalance to industry interventions that may undermine child protections. An individual complaints system would also give children and their parents a way to exercise their rights to protection and provide a mechanism for young users to seek remediation if they come to harm.

The third is to cite the UN Convention on the Rights of the Child and General Comment no. 25 on children's rights in relation to the digital environment. This would support the UK government to fulfil its obligations as a signatory of the Convention and mark a clear commitment to upholding children's rights under the new regime.

2. Protecting children wherever they are online

The new laws will only apply to user-to-user and search services, leaving out platforms that have only provider-generated content, including a number of games and smaller sites that promote life-threatening behaviours, such as eating disorders or self-harm. Children require protection wherever they are online, not only where the government wishes them to be. The legislation will not be future proof if it does not capture all types of services that create risks to children and could encourage services to design their platforms to evade regulation. Already it is unclear if aspects of the Metaverse would fall in scope of the legislation.

The Bill must apply to all services likely to be accessed by children. These services must be subject to the child safety duties and comply with the standards for child safety set out in binding, enforceable codes of practice produced by the regulator.

These recommendations were also put to the government by the Joint Committee on the Draft Online Safety Bill during the pre-legislative scrutiny period. Recognising that not all services that create risk to children were accounted for under the draft legislation, the government did extend the scope, but only to include commercial pornography providers that did not fall under the definition of a user-to-user service. This does not go far enough. All services that create risks to children must be subject to risk assessment and risk mitigation duties. There is an extensive body of research on which both the government and regulator can draw to define these risks and develop related codes. Defining such risks on the face of the Bill is critical to allow Ofcom to begin its work devising a code of practice relating to child online safety, including the steps it expects services to take to effectively eliminate, mitigate and manage such harms.

Services likely to be accessed by children are already in scope of existing children's privacy regulation in the UK, the Age Appropriate Design Code (AADC) (2020), enforced by the Information Commissioner's Office (ICO). Aligning the scope of the Bill with that of the AADC will aid collaboration between the ICO and Ofcom and support companies to comply with their duties to protect children under both parts of the law. Failure to align has been described by both the tech sector and regulators as a potential barrier to good regulatory health that could slow compliance and enforcement action.

3. Tackling child abuse online

Grooming and child abuse images offences are at record levels, and the scale and complexity of the problem grows year-on-year. There has been a 186% increase in child sexual abuse material involving 7–10-year olds since 2020[2].

The Bill must provide the strongest possible response to detect and disrupt preventable online abuse.

It must be strengthened to better respond to the dynamics of the child abuse threat and provide a future-proofed regulatory regime that can effectively tackle preventable online abuse.

Companies must have a duty to identify and counteract pathways to grooming and child abuse that their services facilitate. In particular, they must be compelled to act against child abuse that does not meet the criminal threshold ('child abuse breadcrumbing'). The legislation must also account for the cross-platform nature of harm and demand greater transparency and information sharing between platforms to detect and disrupt abuse.

Ofcom must be given the powers to require the proactive use of technology to detect Child Sexual Exploitation and Abuse (CSEA) to address child abuse in private messages.

When children are contacted by someone they don't know in person, in nearly three quarters (74%) of cases, this contact initially takes place by private message[3]. As the Joint Committee recommended, there must be clear arrangements to detect child abuse material and to ensure the regulator is given the ability to co-designate powers for tackling CSEA, drawing on the expertise of child protection organisations. Co-designation in this area should be explicitly mentioned as an option Ofcom can choose to take on the face of the Bill.

4. Privacy-preserving age assurance

Age assurance is the necessary first step to delivering the protections for children under the Bill. But without a standalone duty that requires services with age restrictions to know the age of their users, the Bill's provisions to protect children will be undermined. This duty must be backed up by a binding code of practice for age assurance that establishes baseline standards of privacy, efficacy and security. Unless there are clear rules of the road for how age assurance systems should be operated, both children and adults will be at risk of excessive and unnecessary data collection, overly restrictive age gating and ineffective or inaccurate age assessments.

Age assurance must be privacy-preserving, effective and fast-tracked to protect children online, with the goal of delivering children the information and experiences that they want and are age-appropriate, not just blocking them out of services or downgrading their experiences.

---

[2] 'Supervise 7-to-10 year-olds online to protect against predators, warn child safety experts', *i*, Jan 11 2022.

[3] NSPCC (2021) Duty to Protect.

The Bill must require services to have secure, privacy-preserving and effective age assurance where it is needed, so children can be given age-appropriate experiences.

Any service with age restrictions, either as required by existing regulations (such as those that apply to gambling service) or as set out in a service's own terms of use, must have proportionate, effective and privacy-preserving age assurance mechanisms in place. To give companies a clear indication of how to achieve this, Ofcom must produce a code of practice for age assurance that sets out rules of the road and establishes expectations for how and when age assurance should be used.

5. Transparency and accountability

The efficacy of the regime will be determined by how it is enforced. Only with robust transparency requirements, clear accountability and a resourced and independent regulator will the government make good on its commitment to make the online world safer for children.

The Bill must demand meaningful transparency and accountability so that companies no longer put profit before children's safety.

Former Facebook employee turned whistle-blower, Frances Haugen, said in her evidence to the Public Bill Committee, "one of the most important things that we need to have in [the Bill] is transparency around how platforms in general, keep children under the age of 13 off their systems and transparency on those processes... that's the single biggest lever in terms of child safety."

As well as transparency around the number of underage users on their platforms, companies must be transparent about the risks to children on their platforms, and particularly the impact of specific functionalities such as algorithmic processing. The Bill must require companies to publish their child risk assessments and give independent researchers access to data so that evolving risks to children can be identified. Companies must also be compelled to publish information about the algorithms used to prioritise, recommend, and moderate content, rank search results and target and profile users. These algorithms are very often the main drivers of harm and the way they are deployed is largely unknown to both users and regulators.

With transparency must come the required regulatory resources and expertise to understand and identify risks to children, to identify appropriate actions and steps to take to mitigate harm, and sufficient enforcement powers to enact those measures. Companies must not be permitted to use commercial sensitivity to avoid transparency obligations, and where there are commercial sensitivities, the regulator must have the power to maintain private oversight.

Without individual director liability, it is hard to see how the largest tech companies, whose enormous wealth and cash reserves can easily absorb even the heaviest fines, will be sufficiently incentivised to comply with their duties. Ofcom should be given powers to issue sanctions against individual company directors for failures to comply with the safety duties under the Bill, and not just for narrow procedural reasons.

Finally, provisions must be made to give bereaved families, coroners, and law enforcement access to data in cases where a child has died or been seriously harmed. The government has stated that the needs of bereaved parents are "outside the scope of this Bill," and despite considerable evidence to the contrary, has asserted that coroners already have the necessary powers to require access to data following the death of a child. This is a truly callous response to the plight of families looking for and routinely denied answers to the circumstances surrounding a child's death.

Conclusion

The Bill presents a singular opportunity to give children long-overdue protections that they deserve, but if these are not fast-tracked, millions of children will not receive the protections they have been promised until they are adults. The children's sector is united in its calls for a fairer, safer, and more equitable online world for children.

We call on the government to accept this package of amendments in its entirety. No single amendment will make the Bill deliver for children, but taken as a whole, these amendments will ensure the government meets its promises to parents and children.

Photo: by Annie Spratt on Unsplash

Listening to Kids – Young Voices on Media Choices

Katie Battersby, Research Executive, KidsKnowBest with
Rebecca Stringer, Research Director, KidsKnowBest

"I prefer on demand… It's just I don't really have the patience for the ads. That's the main bother." *Boy, 14, East Midlands*

Young people are constantly looking for ways to engage with content and would love to have a say in what content and media gets made for them. The future of Public Service Media (PSM) needs to provide an opportunity for young people to explore the world beyond the TV screen – through an Instagram page, behind-the-scenes content, teaser trailers, popular teen actors or relatable storylines. The key is to generate excitement in new ways.

With more children and young people relying on subscription on-demand services as their main outlet to access media, the Children's Media Foundation is working to find out what is pushing them away from linear channels and more traditional television viewing. Children and young people rely on services, such as Netflix, Amazon Prime, Disney+ and YouTube to access their favourite shows and media.

KidsKnowBest contributed to the Children's Media Foundation's PSM campaign by speaking to young people about their TV and on-demand media choices. We explored how young people currently consume their favourite content, their on-demand versus public service usage, and unpacked their views of PSM. Findings were discussed in an online event with panel members, Japhet Asher (Director, Polarity Reversal), Warren Nettleford (Founder, Need to Know) and Dr Jane O'Connor (Reader in Children Studies, Birmingham City University), where we reflected on the importance of the insights on the future of PSM and how it can engage children and young people.

Method

We spoke, in depth, with eight 12–15 year olds from four families with varying viewing habits, who all had an opinion on how best to watch their favourite shows and why. This is the audience most under-served by way of public service content, who have mostly turned to various Subscription Video On Demand (SVOD) platforms to find material that suits their wide-ranging and diverse tastes. Sibling pairs answered eight key questions to gauge their perceptions of PSM and understand personal preferences when it comes to selecting content and channels. After listening to the young people, we had a 30-minute follow-up interview to better understand their behaviours and perceptions.

Findings

Young people are more invested in shows that are watched via on-demand platforms.

> "Mostly by myself I watch streaming services like Netflix and Amazon Prime. You can watch it on any device whenever, wherever you are – and take your pick on what you want to watch."
> *Girl, 14, Cumbria*

Young people's favourite TV shows are found on subscription on-demand platforms. For shows they know and love, they can select specific episodes or seasons for instant gratification, rather than being served whatever is scheduled on linear television. While most of their favourite shows are commissioned by, and shown on SVOD platforms, such as *Stranger Things* (Netflix), some young people love rewatching older shows that they discovered on SVOD platforms, such as *Gilmore Girls* and *Friends*. We would describe the latter as a 'comfort show' because it is familiar, predictable and enjoyable content that lends to solo watching. Young people described these shows as 'escapism' or a chance to unwind from the day.

> "I like watching *Gilmore Girls* on Netflix because it's quite easy to watch and there's not much plot so I can watch it in the background while I do my homework or anything else really." *Girl, 14, Cumbria*

Young people are searching for more content relating to their favourite TV shows.

Not only are young people rewatching their favourite shows on-demand, they are also exploring more content relating to it – whether that is engaging with the actors on social media, liking and sharing relatable memes, watching more of their shows and films, or finding behind the scenes content online.

> "I think I always really love if I know that a movie's come in and it's like in the making. I love to see little snippets of like little behind the scenes videos and all that's got me really excited and engaged. I can't wait for that to come out."
> *Girl, 13, Cumbria*

The content that young people are enjoying on-demand is promoting a 'meta experience' as it lends itself to a world that you can continue to explore, with everything at your fingertips whenever you want it. Young people can become invested in actors, characters, stories, and directors. To improve this age group's engagement in PSM, services need to promote content that can be engaged with across all levels.

Young people watched linear TV when they were young, but now they feel like there is no content that appeals to their age group.

> "BBC I don't really watch much of because the things that it puts on seems to be quite depressing and not something that I generally watch." *Girl, 14, Wales*

Perceptions of linear TV are particularly stunted for young people. 12–15 year olds thought channels such as the BBC represented 'doom and gloom' in the news and more mature content, such as antiques, moving to the countryside, and wildlife documentaries. They recalled watching programmes on Cbeebies, CBBC, CITV when they were much younger, but felt there was nothing commissioned on linear TV to bridge the gap from 'children's TV' to more mature content. There is nothing on there that is made specifically for them.

While young people did associate linear TV channel news with 'doom and gloom', this generation certainly does not shy away from learning about the world they live in. We know that children and young people are engaging with the news in ways that suit their media content habits – through social media platforms in short-form or on-demand documentaries, which tend to be about world issues such as sustainability, endangered species, and inequality.

Linear TV is mainly used for watching showstopper Saturday night programmes.

> "Live TV is quite nice because sometimes they interact with you."
>
> "Yeah and you get that feeling of being included as an audience." *Sisters, 13 & 14, Cumbria*

Types of shows that are better watched with others lend themselves to linear channels, particularly for live TV shows. Those young people that did still watch linear TV, mainly did so to watch family-feel shows at the weekend (e.g. *Strictly, Britain's Got Talent, The Greatest Dancer*), making it a more collective experience, compared to on demand watching. The main pull into watching this content is the interactive nature of watching something live (or as it is being broadcast). With these shows, young people liked that they were always up to date and on trend with the shows they watch, whether that's discussing content with friends or seeing it online.

> "Like with the *Britain's Got Talent* app, you can also vote from there. So you get to interact with it a bit more." *Boy, 12, South and South East England*

Panellist Reflections

During the panel discussion, we presented our insights to the group. Japhet Asher responded by sharing his work on the importance of producing interactive media to engage children and young people in Public Service content. Children and young people are expecting high levels of interaction and engagement with content and would like to have a choice in the content that is served to them on linear channels and in the media beyond. Our findings similarly suggest young people want their voice to be heard when it comes to commissioning new shows on linear TV – this could be done by using social media engagement to generate excitement about new content.

The watching behaviours of children and young people suggest they are more reliant on on-demand services. Dr Jane O'Conner shared her research, suggesting this begins at a very young age. Her research in the watching behaviours of 3–5 year olds showed that children are mostly viewing on demand content on their tablets (YouTube Kids), rather than what would be considered the more traditional way of watching shows – linear channels, such as CBeebies. Furthermore, these children are sophisticated viewers, who are directing themselves and selecting their own content.

With our young people telling us they associate the news on linear channels with 'doom and gloom', young people are sourcing their news from other media outlets, lending itself to solo engagement. Reflecting on the way young people engage with this content, Warren Nettleford spoke about the responsibility of news content to be reliable. Young people need to learn and understand the news on their own, because they are missing out on the conversations that come from watching news with others.

Final thoughts and conclusions

How can linear channels reach out to young people?

Right now, linear TV and on-demand services are serving two different functions – with linear channels being enjoyed as family-centred viewing, and on-demand lending itself to interest driven content selection – but there is no reason these should be mutually exclusive. Linear TV needs to commission shows that are made for young people. Whilst watching scheduled television may not be as flexible, if young people want to fit shows into their busy schedules, they will access it on demand (i.e. iPlayer). They not only need the content there, but they need to *know* that the content is there. The young people we spoke to were not aware of what shows were on live channels and would expect to see adverts or publicity on social channels through the channel or actor pages.

How can we bridge the gap left in the content created for young people?

Reflecting on the shows young people like to watch on-demand, creating storylines that include relatable scenarios or following young people of a similar age to them is important. It is even better if the actors are relatable and have an online presence that the audience can look up to and follow as a way to connect more with the show. If the content is engaging enough, young people are willing to jump channels or platforms to follow their favourite show.

"Millie Bobby Brown. Yeah, she's my favourite of all time." *Girl, 13, Cumbria*

How can content shown on linear channels generate more excitement and exploration?

This process is about building engagement for the audience. Investing in putting more content out there, across social media, for audiences to engage with, to generate excitement around their favourite shows. If their favourite actor or influencer is telling them about something, they will go and find it.

To bridge the gap and create content for this age group, commissioning shows that appeal and resonate with teenagers is important.

To enable a future where children and young people are engaging in PSM, PSM needs to provide media content that is accessible in more than one way – through the TV, on demand, on social media and produce content that resonates with children and young people. Children and young people have an opinion and want to be part of the conversation. The next step is looking at better ways to engage them in content commissioning decisions.

State of the Nation

Dr Rachel Ramsey, Associate Director for Research, Dubit

What do young people think about today's 'big issues'? What influences that thinking? What role, if any, do media play? Kids and youth research agency Dubit set out to answer these questions, and between October and November 2021 interviewed and surveyed more than 500 12–15 year olds across the UK.

We asked them about topics that we think are of major social significance: crime, online privacy and safety, racism, diversity, climate change, gender equality, and social media. The findings indicated a population that cares and worries about these issues, and many young people feel affected by them.

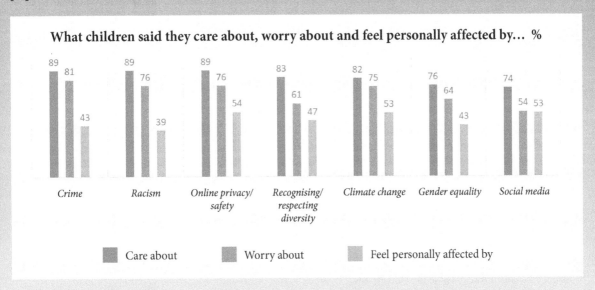

The majority were confident that they knew enough about the topics we explored, tending to cite TV news, family, friends and teachers as sources that influenced their thinking. Of those who don't think they know enough, most want to know more; however, not all felt they had the time. We therefore need to design an intervention that better enables young people to learn about societal issues. Crucially, this intervention must accommodate existing demands on young people's time and intellectual bandwidth.

Young people are under great pressure to develop socially, emotionally, and intellectually; consequently free time is in short supply. Maintaining relationships and friendships – in the park, in messaging, social media or gaming – is essential for social development. Time out – to relax, pursue hobbies, exercise – is critical in maintaining and enhancing emotional wellbeing. School and homework are critical to the intellectual development they'll need to be independent in adulthood;

more immediately, they're critical to getting good grades, which 61% of 12–15 year olds worry about. Alongside these pressures is widely-held concern about societal challenges and a desire to understand them more. A 14 year old interviewee prompted us to consider the conflict between learning about something as important as climate change, and meeting educational demands and expectations:

> "I don't think [climate change] bothers us enough. I know that something has to be done about it because I've learned about it at school, all the effects that it is having but like I'm more bothered about my homework that is due tomorrow."
> Girl, 14, Gateshead

She elegantly captures this conflict and her statement poses an intriguing question: why does she feel that doing her homework is more important than taking action about climate change? Of course, it reflects her commitment to doing well at school. However, it also reflects the fact that this societal challenge and academic challenges run in parallel.

Our survey revealed that more young people want to learn about almost all of these issues from teachers than any other source. However, that need is currently underserved; for example, 28% of 12–15 year olds say that teachers influence how they think and feel about climate change, yet 45% of those who want to know more say that they want to learn about it from teachers.

The importance of the role of education in supporting young people to learn about societal issues cannot be understated. However, our findings suggest that it is currently unable to meet demand, and others have drawn similar conclusions. For example, a recent Ofsted report describes widespread inadequacies in teaching relationships, sex and health education (Ofsted 2021); likewise educational institutions and pupils have called for action on colonialism in curricula at all educational levels, whether by requiring schools to teach children about Britain's role in colonisation and the transatlantic slave trade, or by decolonising curricula.

There is no single means of reaching all young people; moreover some of those means of informing young people about 'big issues', such as friends and family, are not open to the type of external influence needed to improve young people's understanding of topics. Instead, more can be reached through strategic coordination across multiple sources. The chart below aggregates the proportion of survey respondents who want to learn about a topic via a particular source, and illustrates the relative popularity of three combinations of externally-influenceable sources.

This data shows how we might enable young people to learn about these topics, and the gains in reach achieved by distributing content more widely. For example, 65% of those who want to know more about climate change said that they want to learn about it from TV and/or teachers. Adding YouTube increases the reach by 4%; adding streaming services would bump that to 71%. Naturally, the more sources used, the greater the expense; as the data for crime and social media indicate, more sources do not necessarily lead to wider reach.

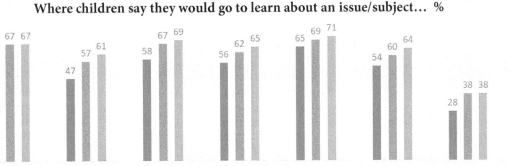

Where children say they would go to learn about an issue/subject... %

TV and Teachers TV, Teachers and YouTube TV, Streaming, Teachers and YouTube
(Aggregate sources of information)

This reveals an opportunity to re-harness the combined reach of media and teaching to enable young people to learn about these issues throughout their school lives. The chart above indicates that by combining teachers with broadcast TV, and perhaps other media, more young people will be able to access learning about these topics in a way they find engaging than if only the most popular source (typically teachers) is used.

There is another, more practical reason for pairing teaching with media. The shortcomings in teaching about these issues emerge not simply from gaps in the curriculum; there are myriad factors, including an emphasis on passing exams rather than broader learning, teacher training, and access to – and capacity to adapt to – new knowledge, for example developments in climate science. In other words, these shortcomings result from educational policy, which is a slow-moving beast and, if it were to change, that change would take time. In the meantime, and beyond, the media could play a substantial role in delivering informative, credible and engaging content for use in schools and other educational settings, and the home. It might even complement curricula for teacher education programmes. Of course, this concept is not new. John Richmond recounts the role of the Broadcasting Act 1990 and successive legislation in mandating publicly-funded broadcasters to deliver educational content. More recently, when the Covid pandemic resulted in school closures, the BBC delivered an expansive programme of educational TV and online content used by teachers and families. Some of this drew on the broadcaster's vast catalogue of content but new shows and educational materials were also produced, despite the logistical challenges of producing new material while maintaining social distancing.

Young people are demonstrably concerned about and feel affected by these topics, and many want to know more about them. We asked them where they want to learn about them, and they told us. If we are to enable young people to understand and contribute to society, and understand and help to address its biggest challenges, we must invest in the sources they ask for: education, and broadcast TV (with a bit of YouTube).

Young People as **Change Makers**

Gemma Robinson, Community Development Manager, Thred Media

Thred Media is a social enterprise focused on publishing, consulting, and production. The central arm of the business is our social change-focused web publication thred.com, which features daily coverage and analysis on all aspects of youth culture seen through the lens of social change. Every story, written by our global team of Gen Z writers, must have a 'thred' of positive social change to make the cut.

We launched our Change Maker Network in 2021 in order to provide opportunities for Gen Z who would like to make connections in social and environmental change movements, lead global discussions and gain planet-positive experience in the workplace. The Network is now a vast and close-knit community of young people we work with every day, with the aim of making a real impact on the world in the areas that matter to them most.

The Children's Media Yearbook asked our global Change Makers, what change would have the biggest positive impact on their community?

I would love to see an improvement to the education system of Indonesia, especially so it is more inclusive of students with disabilities. Currently, students with disabilities are made to attend segregated schools and are isolated from their peers, and a shockingly low number of young people with disabilities actually attend school at all. Teachers must modify their materials, methods, instructions, and assessments to meet all students' diverse learning needs. *Maria Florensia Chandra, 16, Indonesia*

Ecuador has always been known for its beautiful natural landscape. However, most of the country's income is based on petroleum, which destroys the environment. Despite it being so harmful, the government sees money and profit as being more important than limiting the land petrol companies use, which could prevent national parks and animal species from being destroyed. This is the area I'd most like to see change in.
Daniella Martinez, 16, Ecuador

When I was growing up, I noticed gender discrimination a lot. I saw women doing household chores and obeying men, while the men spent time outside the house and disrespected women. It was assumed that women should not take part in higher education, especially in scientific fields, and consent was not taken seriously. When I started to ask older people about these things I was told that's just how it works. From an early age I felt the need to protest and, though we face a lot of obstacles, I believe we will achieve gender equality one day and make the world a better place, free from all kinds of discriminative behaviours. *Rubaiya Shanjidah, 16, Bangladesh*

The most important area that I want to see change in is the stigma around mental health. Personally, I rarely speak about mental health to my family because they don't always address it in a positive way, believing that Gen Z opening up about their struggles makes them 'weak'. This experience is common among young people and needs to change. *Kaylie Athena Pangestoe, 14, Indonesia*

As a young person growing up in Nigeria, improved access to quality education could have drastically improved the lives of those in my community. The changes I'd most like to see could come in the form of scholarships, learning materials and facilities. With these, children can find encouragement to learn and successfully become our future leaders. *Patience Adesominu, 18, Nigeria*

Growing up, I would have liked to see climate and the earth take a more central role in learning, right the way through from primary school. I think it would be less challenging to live sustainably if awareness is increased at a younger age, so positive changes to lifestyle can be implemented earlier. If this were the case then living a sustainable life would feel natural as you mature, and interest would be increased to enhance it even further as you learn more. *Palmer Newson, 17, United Kingdom*

The population of India is growing at an extraordinary rate. There are over 100 million people between the ages of 15 and 19 but not nearly as many jobs, creating an employment crisis for the youth – especially in the technology industry. Those that have the means to move or study abroad have better prospects when it comes to living conditions, education and employment, but everyone else is left behind. The air pollution has been so bad the past few years that schools and highways have had to close in the winter, and there have been record breaking temperatures in the summer. It's hard to specify one change because I believe that everything is related. It may take time, but I do continue to hope that improvements will happen in my country. *Shipra Singh, 16, India*

I would like the Azerbaijani education system to meet all international standards. Unfortunately, this kind of education is currently only available in private schools and as a result, public school students cannot directly apply to most European universities. Furthermore, school students can only study in Azerbaijani or Russian languages, however, it would be great if there was an English sector as well. *Aysu Ahmad, 17, Azerbaijan*

A lot of girls growing up in India face problems because of limited access to menstrual hygiene products, education, and equal rights. I believe women are equally strong as men and need to be empowered for the world to be a better place. This can be achieved by putting an end to early marriages and ensuring girls go to school instead, giving them equal rights to boys, as well as proper access to menstrual hygiene products.
Affreen Parveen, 17, India

WHAT CMF DOES IS IMPORTANT WORK

The way our children see themselves reflected across their media experiences is fundamental in defining their view of the world, their values and their aspirations.

This is why the Children's Media Foundation has never been more important and we are incredibly proud to support the brilliant work you do.

Keep doing it.

The Metaverse: Words of Definition and Caution on the Word of the Year

Japhet Asher, Director, Polarity Reversal

Via his film *La Chinoise*, Jean Luc Godard suggested we should view the work of Méliès, the first fantasy filmmaker, and the Lumière Brothers, the first documentarians, the other way round. You can argue that the Lumières, by placing their camera down and choosing what to film, were changing reality around them, whereas Méliès, in his use of special effects and trick photography, was documenting the underside of the mind. The current debate about the Metaverse reminds me of this critique of our earliest filmmakers. The first filmmakers shared tools in common – cameras, film stock, projectors – much as digital makers across AR and VR today share game engines and 3D models. Remember that audiences reacted viscerally to the Lumières' train leaving the station as though it might hit them through the screen and perceived black and white scenes from life as the same kind of magical vision that Méliès offered with his trip to the moon. But their goals and storytelling techniques could not have been more different. We are in the equivalent of these early filmmaking days with AR and VR now, a long way from a maturing medium and discovering the *Citizen Kane* of VR narrative or the *Sesame Street* of AR early learning. Everything is shiny and new – we will go through many cool experiments, gimmicks and spectacles to uncover what sticks and is genuinely useful/joyful in these emerging media.

People regularly conflate AR and VR, which is strange to me, given that the two serve contradictory purposes. AR is anchored to physical objects in the real world, whereas the goal of VR is to remove the user from their physical surroundings and immerse them in an alternate digital reality. They are diametrically opposed. So it's no wonder that there is even greater debate and misunderstanding over the Metaverse.

Like it or not, 'Metaverse' has been made the word of the year. I don't much care for the word at all, but we seem to be stuck with it for now (thanks, Zuck). So let's start with some definitions. The term Metaverse was famously coined by Neal Stephenson in his 1992 novel *Snow Crash* and was created to refer to a single 3D virtual world mapped over the real world. Many people focus on the first element only, thinking of the Metaverse as being all about VR and online virtual worlds like *Fortnite* and *Roblox*, and the possibility that some day you might move seamlessly between such worlds with your self defined virtual identity and resources, whether to a game session, a work meeting or a virtual marketplace. Of course, this requires an underlying infrastructure that current virtual worlds only offer in their own games.

Others use the Metaverse as a much broader catch-all for the range of technologies emerging around Web 3, 5G and the blockchain, NFTs and photogrammetry, as well as AR and VR. We are told that these developments will deliver a newly democratic 3D internet with a creator led content/experience economy and open access for all and provide the backbone for journeys across virtual worlds.

(A side note: Those of us who remember the early days of the web will note the worryingly familiar utopian magical thinking here. After all, underlying all of this technology is the power of cloud servers, machine learning and AI. And megacorporations with massive, competing interests.)

Both views above are valid, but I prefer to think of the Metaverse as a series of digital layers over our physical world, layers we might choose to access based on context.

The internet we know is built on connected devices. The Metaverse and Web 3 will also use contextual or semantic computing and spatial imaging that combine to paint our physical world with 3D digital data – whether invisible (object recognition/mapping), translucent (AR information and customisation) or transformational (VR and virtual worlds) – and deliver content shaped by context.

Imagine some layers you can't see that speak to machines, like self driving cars; layers that you can see in real world space – say, the archive of the BBC deployed to enhance public spaces with location relevant AR content, or fashion designers making digital elements to enhance your appearance; fully immersive layers in VR that transform the limits of your living room walls into a spatial expanse for learning new skills or playing with friends from across the globe. All of these layers are possible in some form with today's technology – and much more is to come.

The engines of this new era come primarily from games and 3D graphics companies – for example, Epic's Unreal Engine, the mobile 3D engine Unity and the *Pokémon Go* creator's, Niantic. But these game engines' objectives aren't just about games. Through its users' gameplay, Niantic is mapping the world around us, scanning and 'owning' our landscapes. Unreal is providing deeply realistic 3D tools and environments for uses that range from training humans to designing cars, delivering visual effects, as well as fighting fantasms. Real time virtual events can be delivered via the engine, not just in *Fortnite*, but in custom built environments, along with the advertising and merchandise that go with them. Unity is aiming to give digital objects the same 'rights' as physical ones, uniting with apps like Sketchfab to offer any physical asset its digital twin. These platforms may have their roots in gameplay, and that will persist, but the layers of the Metaverse they are building will cut across almost every use case you can imagine. Eventually.

Photo: Ars Electronica / Martin Hieslmair on Flickr

The technology to support the Metaverse (whatever your definition) is inevitable, but hardware and software will take more time to develop than many realise. The other major question mark is about human behaviour.

Do most people want to spend work, social and personal time in a virtual construct? At the moment, gamers are the early adopters of VR technology. Will the rest of us follow?

It's worth noting that Snapchat have been determinedly focused on the present or near present. Take a look at their recent Spectacles demo video for a glimpse of what's already possible with their AR glasses and the range of use cases they are exploring. AR glasses from Meta are coming soon, and the Lens studio model from Snap has quickly become core to Instagram and TikTok creators. They are banking on real world experiences you can share with friends and family enhanced or even defined by digital overlays. And in May, Google opened up its Streetview maps for AR creators to anchor their work in any physical location shown.

So what does all this mean for children? Many cheerleaders promote VR for kids without fully recognising the difference between an explorable world on a computer versus an immersive experience via a headset. Many parents ignored the 13+ advice on headsets in their purchases for their families last Christmas. While playing a round of *Beat Saber* might pose little risk, there are few safe spaces for children in existing social VR environments and almost no coherent moderation. Devices aren't being designed yet for a child's physiognomy and equally there is

little research on the potential impact on mental development of exposure to VR experiences at an age when perception of the real world is still malleable. For all the immense potential of VR to deliver amazing edtech learning journeys, more research is urgently needed in this area. At the same time, we need to recognise, like training a young mind to control the Force and become a Jedi, that some form of the Metaverse will be a huge part of our children's lives, so we need to let them embrace what it offers as soon as is appropriate.

AR provides an easier and safer on-ramp. In my own work, I've found that AR overlays mean little to very early learners – the world is full of surprises and things to discover for them, and all five senses need to be engaged in that process. But once their brains have grasped abstractions like symbols on a page forming language that they can understand and share, AR overlays on the real world can fit coherently into their mental landscape. They understand the rules and behaviour of physical objects and symbols. They have a context into which AR can be placed to support play, social interaction and learning without undermining cognition.

I'm exploring an AR use case that has potential value for kids and adults. I'm bringing the Metaverse to books. Here's what I've learned.

A book is a platform for stories, images and a mental projection from author to reader – Stephen King describes writing as a way for described objects and people to travel through time and space from his desk to your living room – telepathy. But a book is much more than that. It's a physical object that has visceral qualities and can become talismanic for a reader – we keep them on our shelves because we value them as objects as well as containers. They become badges of our identity. Books are consumed in a context – a place, a time, a state of mind that changes the way we perceive them and the role they play in our lives. We live with books, we use them, we touch them – we don't just watch them. They trigger our own thoughts, emotions and memories as well as containing those of their authors and we see them as cherished objects as a result. As we build a bridge to digital tools from physical books we can unleash all that stored potential of emotion and interaction.

So I'm building the bridge between physical books and digital tools to empower active readers, social readers, engaged learners, puzzlers, thinkers and creators. Always remembering that by putting down your device, or taking off your smart glasses (when we have them), you can also just focus on the ink and texture of words and pictures beautifully printed on physical paper in all its time tested simplicity and glory.

I actually think that's a microcosm of how we will feel about the Metaverse as a whole – it will be there for you when it is what you need or want. But you'll also need to be able to switch it off and just look for shapes in clouds, hold hands or read a good book.

Whatever your definition of the Metaverse, I suspect Neal Stephenson would agree that stories in books already spark the best Metaverse of all, owned by none but ourselves: the one in our imagination. And right now we can still imagine the Metaverse is anything we want it to be.

Photo: Ars Electronica / Martin Hieslmair on Flickr

"This is New, Surely It's Dangerous!?"

Prof Andy Phippen, Professor of Digital Rights, Bournemouth University

Early in 2022, I woke and, as is typical, I checked various news sites to see what has been happening in the world. One particular article caught my attention. On the BBC News website, I saw the headline 'Metaverse app allows kids into virtual strip clubs' (Crawford and Smith, 2022). The article continued to explain that a reporter "posing as a 13 year old girl witnessed grooming, sexual material, racist insults and a rape threat in the virtual-reality world!" Within the article there were accusations that the platform used was "dangerous by design" and "a toxic combination of risks." Clearly (or at least, clearly from this article), this emerging Metaverse is dangerous!

I have spent over 15 years researching the impact of digital technology upon society, in particular children and young people, looking at issues of social policy, law and technology. Over this time I have spoken to thousands of young people about their online lives, their concerns, and how their lives are intertwined with digital technology (for example see Phippen and Street, 2022). What generally emerges from these conversations is an enthusiasm for digital technology, and a passion for whatever they see as 'their' digital world. They also have concerns, and we talk about these a lot. These tend, in the main, to be around interactions with peers and online friendships.

I also speak to other stakeholders, such as the media and politicians. Generally, an opening question is "This <new technology>, what are the harms and how can they be stopped?" (Not an exhaustive lists, but I can recall being asked this about MSN, MySpace, Bebo, Facebook, Ask.FM, WhatsApp, Snapchap, Instagram, *Call of Duty*, *Grand Theft Auto*, *Fortnite*, *Among Us*, Pornhub, Tinder, *Minecraft*, *Roblox*, and the Metaverse. There are many, many others that I cannot recall at the time of writing.)

Clearly, at the moment, this 'concern' lies in the harms potentially caused by the Metaverse.

The emerging Online Safety Bill, announced by the government:

marks a milestone in the fight for a new digital age which is safer for users and holds tech giants to account.

It focuses on the need for platforms to adopt a duty of care model which mitigates risk of harm to their users. However, the Bill has little clarity in terms of what might constitute harm, or risk mitigation; this is something that platforms need to examine or demonstrate, rather than definitions being prescribed. It's an interesting model of technology regulation, which perhaps future-proofs the legislation, but it is all somewhat intangible and encourages vague accusations of companies not caring or being "dangerous by design."

Returning to the BBC News article, it named the platform the journalist was using, so I took the liberty of checking out their website and explored the tools that they provide to mitigate risk upon their platform. Unsurprisingly, they had routes for disclosure and reporting abusive users, and tools for muting and blocking. However, none of this was reported in the article.

This leads me to the question – what more can the platform do? Is this really a "toxic combination of risk?" Or does this article paint the end user as passive: saying "I used this thing and bad things happened, this means the thing is bad?"

While I am not generally a fan of road safety analogies in this context, here I will use one. While we expect the manufacturers of motor vehicles to provide tools that allow us to mitigate risk on the road (steering, brakes, etc.), there is also a role for other stakeholders – for example, the driver themselves should not simply jump into a car and, after driving it into a ditch, shout "How can Skoda allow this to happen!?"

In considering what more platforms can do to demonstrate their duty of care, policy makers and many with child protection concerns might view artificial intelligence as the solution to these issues. "Surely," they say, "these clever tech people can use things like artificial intelligence in their algorithms to make sure harms don't occur!?" But there is one group of people not proposing intangibly defined AI solutions to prevent these harms – the clever tech people.

Photo: by Emily Wade on Unsplash

The idea that a system could be established that could, in real time, scan all of the interactions that are occurring on a platform and make subjective interpretations around the intentions of those involved in the interaction, and prevent an end user, again in real time, from expressing an offensive view, is a pipe dream.

So, instead, put-upon companies, threatened with stronger and stronger regulation, do all they can do, which are familiar, well-established technologies, such as keyword matching and hashlists, alongside attempts at natural language processing, built on corpuses of previously disclosed and moderated abuse. Which sometimes works, but probably also accounts for growing frustration with social media users around warnings or suspensions for an innocuous phrase that happened to include an 'abusive' keyword or phrase. I have asked colleagues who work for these platforms to remind their developers that 'Plymouth Hoe' is a location, not a derogatory term for a resident.

I am reminded, once again, of the somewhat famous quote by cybersecurity researcher Marcus Ranum:

You do not solve social problems with software.

Clearly, platforms have a role to play in ensuring that users understand the risks associated with using their products and how to mitigate them. (I far prefer the term 'risk mitigation' to 'online safety'. Safety implies "free of harm or risk of harm," which is a pipe dream in any user-to-user communication scenario, regardless of online or offline.) And the looming Online Safety Bill has some value in making providers think about these risks and demonstrate they have considered them.

However, in talking to young people, many have called for better education, the means to be able to ask questions (and get answers) and, perhaps the thing I have heard the most – a wish that, whether at home or in school, they can disclose harms and get support. I have never heard a young person call for the government to "bring big tech billionaires to heel."

Yes, they expect platforms to provide the means to manage interactions and provide the tools to block and report harmful behaviour (and show that complaints are listened to). Yet if one is to explore the Online Safety Bill, there is barely a mention on education. Platforms can 'do more', but they can also only do so much. Other stakeholders need to play their part too.

References

Phippen, A., & Street, L. (2022) *Online Resilience and Wellbeing in Young People*. Palgrave Macmillan.

Crawford, A and Smith, T. (2022) 'Metaverse app allows kids into virtual strip clubs'. *BBC News*, February 23. https://www.bbc.co.uk/news/technology-60415317

Play Across Worlds

 Dr Jane Mavoa, Postdoctoral Researcher, University of Melbourne

During the covid pandemic children have had to adapt their play to a reduced range of physical environments. While there are now well justified and much needed pushes to get kids playing outside, over the last couple of years we have had an opportunity to pay more attention to what it is they get up to in their *digital* playworlds. My research (conducted prior to the pandemic) looked at young children's play in *Minecraft* and was motivated by the large amounts of words written and time spent worrying about the effects of children's videogames – and the comparatively scant attention paid to what play in games like *Minecraft* actually *is*. I found that children engaged in a wide range of different types of play, including creating structures, experimenting with making machines, joking around with siblings or parents and role-playing.

Children worked with, or around, the limitations of the digital environment to construct moments of play that were in many cases analogous to play that may happen without any digital component at all. One of the more striking things that I noticed when watching children play *Minecraft* was the ways in which play traversed both the physical spaces of living rooms and bedrooms and the on-screen world simultaneously. *Minecraft* play was not disconnected from the immediate social and physical surrounds of children's homes. Indeed, in many cases there were clear connections with other forms of play, creative outlets or general interests.

One child, James (pseudonym) aged 6, was very interested in playing 'schools' at the time of my research. His bedroom contained both a whiteboard and a blackboard, delineating space for playing 'schools' away from his Lego box, book collection, and red racing car shaped bed. James and his father explained that sometimes James played 'schools' on his own with students from his imagination, and other times with family members, including grandparents and the family dog. In this play, James would pretend to be the teacher and deliver various lessons with his obliging 'students' following instructions (to the best of their respective abilities).

But James's interest in playing schools carried over to his *Minecraft* worlds. One world he showed me was particularly relevant here. It was strikingly colourful, containing numerous structures, of varying sizes, designed for a range of purposes, all having taken a lot of time and effort to create. But of all the structures in this fantastical metropolis it was the school building that most caught my attention. Here, James pointed out classrooms for different year levels and, replicating his real school, spots marked on the ground for pupils to line up after play time ("all the classes line up here, when the play is finished," he explains). The school was very much a work in progress with James telling me of his grand plans for a swimming pool and perhaps extensions to some of the classrooms. However, in a departure from both his real school and the pretend school in his bedroom, *this* one included secret passageways, pools of lava hidden behind the walls and the opportunity to visualise and construct an almost limitless range of structures – and therefore possibilities. James was the author and director of his play as it occurred across physical and digital worlds. In the physical environment of his bedroom, he had whiteboards and willing participants to act as students. In the digital environment he had secret passageways, lava tunnels and the ability to visualise, plan, and construct whatever it was that he wanted this school to be.

What this demonstrates is the fluidity of play across physical and digital spaces that many scholars have noted, but that still seems to be forgotten about when we find ourselves worrying about whether our children have possibly spent a little too long engrossed in 'the screen'. From observing *Minecraft* play as it happened in amongst busy household comings and goings, and as it was shaped by children's general interests, other forms of play, and in-the-moment desires, it was clear that rather than being cut off from the rest of the world, children were in fact inhabiting multiple worlds at once. And their play in each was held together by an overarching imaginary and individual agency. The digital and physical spaces that children manipulate via imagination during the course of play each have their own unique

Photo: by Kelly Sikkema on Unsplash

limitations, risks and possibilities, which children work with, or work around, to produce meaningful moments of play.

Recently we've been hearing a lot about the metaverse. While there's some confusion about what exactly the metaverse will be, it seems to potentially be a place for adults to hang out, play and work in a multiplicity of spaces – similar to the ways that children play across spaces – but with the addition of virtual and augmented reality devices designed to produce a more sensorily rich experience. It is interesting that so many of the examples used in speculation about what the metaverse might be involve play and games.

There are of course less-fun aspects of both digital playworlds inhabited by children and the metaverse – the need for various stakeholders to make money, and the intrusion of commercial interests into these spaces, is just one example. But there are similarities here, too. Having your virtual avatar dressed well in the metaverse may involve a very similar kind of shopping experience as children trying on virtual outfits in *Minecraft* or *Roblox*. Although, where children may badger their parents to spend

'real' money on in-game currency to buy these outfits, the metaverse will involve an economic system based around cryptocurrency and the trading of digital artefacts, both of which have received a range of critiques.

It will be interesting to see how the metaverse evolves. Will it retain the playfulness that at present seems to define it (at least in all the marketing and hype)? Or, as I suspect is more likely, will commercial imperatives and other adult concerns come to dominate in such a way that any similarities with the playfulness of digital spaces inhabited by children give way almost entirely to consumption and work?

Either way, as we emerge cautiously from our pandemic bubbles, it is worth reflecting on how children's play has adapted to include digital spaces, not necessarily having been replaced by them. Now might also be a good time to ask ourselves: what might we learn from observing children's digital play, and the hopes and concerns surrounding it, as tech giants push forward with blurring the boundaries in ever greater parts of our lives between the digital and the physical?

References

Burn, A. (2013) Computer games on the playground: Ludic systems, dramatized narrative and virtual embodiment. In R. Willett, J. Bishop, J. Marsh, & C. Richards, *Children, Media and Playground Cultures: Ethnographic studies of school playtimes* (pp. 120–144). Palgrave MacMillan.

Fleer, M. (2014) The demands and motives afforded through digital play in early childhood activity settings. *Learning Culture and Social Interaction*, 3(3), 202–209.

Giddings, S. (2014a) *Gameworlds: Virtual media and children's everyday play*. Bloomsbury.

Reflecting on **Youth Mental Health** and Tech Regulation in Anticipation of the Metaverse

Prof Sonia Livingstone, Professor of Social Psychology, LSE

Whistle-blower Frances Haugen's revelation that Facebook (as was) had held back research showing that the company was aware that using Instagram can damage girls' mental health triggered a widespread debate over tech platforms' responsibility, especially for vulnerable children. The research turned out not to be so robust, and the findings were hardly surprising to the research community, given the established debate over the (still-contested) link between social media and youth wellbeing. In this multi-stakeholder and highly contested domain, social scientists have sought ways to counter moral and media panics, transcend polarised debates and gather robust evidence that can guide the way forward.

But the challenge remains as to how we can recognise and address the problem of mental health among youth in a digital age. Two questions are particularly difficult to answer:

1. How shall we apportion responsibility for digitally-mediated risks of harm between platforms, government, public services and the public?
2. How should we balance the needs of 'vulnerable' minorities against the freedoms of the majority of internet users?

Framing the problem

On the question of responsibility, I suggest that even in these days of social media, much policy and public debate tacitly assumes a Web 1.0 world in which communication operates on a pull, not push, basis – a world where users make choices, wise or not, about sites to visit, images to look at, communities to join. The talk is often still of '*the* online domain' rather than the *multiple* and highly personalised online worlds that diverse groups experience, being differently targeted (arguably discriminated against) by platforms using a host of commercially-driven push and nudge strategies based on sorting people's feeds, pathways or bubbles.

This makes it easier to fall into the trap of victim-blaming talk or, more subtly, talk that puts the responsibility on young internet users and demands their constant resilience.

On weighing the status of minority audiences, and setting aside the fact that if you add them up, they constitute a majority, it remains tempting for policymakers to assume 'average' or 'typical' users. Even from researchers, having read (and contributed to some of) the evidence reviews showing the uncertain relation between youth mental health and digital engagement, I am becoming uneasy at the 'on the one hand, on the other hand' conclusions that can seem to reproduce attention to the 'average user' rather than those – however few – who are distinctively at risk online.

So, I welcome the emerging critique of platform policies and design that seeks to make visible the diversity of actual users living contextually specific lives. This critique builds on a long tradition of work on imagined versus empirical audiences and textually inscribed or real-life readers, as well on the increasing calls for by-design solutions – safety-by-design, privacy-by-design, security-by-design and – important in my work – child-rights-by-design.

Such moves are intended to counter the ways in which platforms can be seen as deliberately risky-by-design, driven by exploitative business models, designed to evade regulation, realised through opaque affordances, with minimal provision for rights or remedy. Especially highlighting the operation of algorithms, we now hear everywhere the metaphor of falling 'down the rabbit hole', though Instagram or TikTok or the many others, are hardly delivering 'a wonderland' for *some* young people.

Listening to children's lived experiences

It seems increasingly urgent to counter the 'outsider voices' currently dominating the debate (whether government, policymakers, industry, worried parents or panicky media) with 'insider insights' (especially children and young people's voices, representing the lived experiences of diverse cultures both on and offline).

In recent work for the EU-funded ySKILLS project, my colleagues and I have been interviewing adolescents with mental health problems about their lived experiences and digital engagement:

- A 16 year old, in therapy for past experiences of sexual abuse, tells us of someone "doing a TikTok live and he had killed himself in TikTok … and that ended up on people's pages and people were reposting it."

Photo: by bruce mars on Unsplash

- A 17 year old with a bipolar diagnosis: "when I am in a manic, I'm pretty sure I just send random shit to people."
- A 17 year old with experience of an eating disorder and domestic abuse told us how, "If you're on TikTok, what you mostly do is you send them a link of a Twitter one… And then if you go onto the Twitter link, then if Twitter takes down the video, they'll just send you a link of this app called Dropbox, which downloads any illegal video. And you can either just download it or they'll DM it and you can access it."
- A 14 year old with a problematic relation with food: "in lockdown, people were doing… 'what I eat in a day'. I think the algorithm or something changed for me. My whole feed was just full of 'what I eat in a day'… I'm like 12, thinking about it. I eat three meals, and then these people are having a strawberry for brunch, and that was a big thing."
- A suicidal 18 year old: "it's naked children on a social media. They don't have the choice. People are getting hold of people's photos… Someone's gone out their way, without their permission, to post photos. It destroys people's lives. Honestly, it's vile."

To many adults, it may seem as if "she/he's always staring at the phone." But what's happening on that phone can be dramatic to the young person and invisible to observers. Yet much of it is visible to the platforms, so what should they be doing differently?

Ways of thinking, ways ahead

In the child rights space, we're seeing growing recognition of the importance of respecting a child's best interests. This means attending holistically to the specific balance of factors that shapes their world. But can we figure out how the best interests of the child can be respected in digital environments, when platforms say they don't even know who is a child online, let alone their mental health status or offline risk or support structures? Can we design with children's best interests in mind?

While I was thinking about all of this, over the past year or so, a new debate suddenly hit the headlines: the Metaverse! As major companies get excited about the Metaverse – as if *Second Life*, *Habbo Hotel*, *Club Penguin* never happened, and never went wrong for kids – again, thorny questions arise about how the affordances of the digital amplify, exacerbate, perpetuate and intensify some harms in ways that merit attention and intervention. And about how to protect the needs and human rights of vulnerable users.

It seems urgent that we find ways to recognise vulnerability, even as we fully acknowledge that children are agents, actors, citizens, not just victims in need of protection. After all, online and offline, they are not living in circumstances of their own making, some have had a lot to contend with, and the power of platforms dwarfs the agency of even privileged and resilient groups.

I also find it helpful to continue to refer to online and offline, even as I fully acknowledge that the digital is fast becoming infrastructural in society, and that young people move seamlessly across multiple environments without marking the difference. This is because I don't think we've got to the bottom of how there are problematic disjunctures in visibility, power and design across those environments. Or of how, although mental health difficulties result from many circumstances unrelated to technology, the established supports in place in our homes, schools, neighbourhoods and public services are being disintermediated and disrupted by digital innovations.

We must also keep in mind that, in asking how to mitigate the risk of harm, we do not forget that digital innovation offers young people many opportunities, including access to vital sources of help, that all risk does not result in harm, and that some exposure to risk is needed to build resilience.

In these short reflections, I can only pose, not answer, the big questions with which I began.

Recognising that multiple stakeholders must share the responsibility in multiple ways, it remains difficult to figure out what can be done about the digital platforms – without returning to the old

binary of child protection versus adult freedom of expression (as if children do not also need and have the right to freedom of expression, and as if many adults are not also calling for greater protection online). And without seeming to promote tech solutionism or being panned as techno-determinists. One way forward is to take a child rights-approach, working with UN human and child rights organisations, since this approach prioritises human rights due diligence for business in ways that are accountable to governments.

It's beginning to seem urgent that we collate our evidence, critical arguments and calls for action in anticipation of the Metaverse.

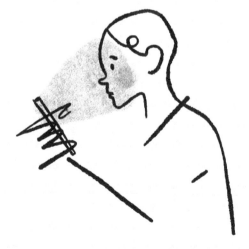

Three Stones Media

DEVELOPING, DELIVERING & INSPIRING SINCE 2007

The Children's Media
FOUNDATION

threestonesmedia.com
intouch@threestonesmedia.com
1 Battersea Square, London SW11 3RZ

KINDLE ENTERTAINMENT
4 X 30' FOR SKY KIDS & 1 X 90' FOR SKY CINEMA

Jacqueline Wilson's
LITTLE DARLINGS

FINALIST

BROADCAST DIGITAL AWARDS 2022

WILD SEED STUDIOS

DODO

Welcome back to Sheffield everyone. It's great to see you all again!

WILDSEEDSTUDIOS.COM

Closing the Word Gap Through Film

Jo Claessens, Series Producer, BBC Education

One in four children start primary school without basic literacy skills, a figure that rises to one in three[1] in some parts of the UK. Research tells us that being unable to communicate effectively at school could limit your life chances. So what is needed to reduce this 'word gap' … and how can the BBC play a part in helping parents boost their child's language?

This was the starting point for the creation of the BBC's most ambitious education service for parents of 0–4 year olds. *Tiny Happy People*, launched by the Duchess of Cambridge on BBC Breakfast, has a simple message at its heart – talk to your baby as much as possible from birth. The mission is to show *how* and, most importantly, why this is so essential to children's development. The free website is packed with tips and advice from healthcare practitioners, expert child development content and hundreds of short parent-led films with easy to follow activities to do at home.

Making the research accessible

Getting to this point has been a journey. We started with a problem we wanted to solve and we knew we needed to immerse ourselves in the world of speech, language and communication from the start. Which is how, as Series Producer, I found myself in a room with brilliant

academics, experts in speech and language therapy and senior healthcare practitioners.

Our first step was interpreting the academic terms, practitioner insights, and the evidence-based research to do with child language development and figuring out which of these 'essential ingredients' to communicate to parents and how. How could we create films that were accessible, inspiring *and* showcased simple techniques parents could use at home to support their little ones' language development?

Casting is key

The next focus was finding relatable families to appear in our films. We want *Tiny Happy People* to be an inclusive resource. From LGBTQ+ parents, to families raising multilingual children, to being a parent with disabilities – we want all parents to see themselves reflected in our films and articles.

Our USP is that we always work with real

---

[1] Department for Education, 2019, with a similar picture across all nations of the UK.

parents, so many of our families are found by street casting and on social media rather than casting agencies. *Tiny Happy People* is for all parents, we are always supportive, our messages are positive and respectful and we have a duty of care that we take very seriously.

Ages and stages

Another challenge we've faced is filming babies and children. As I'm sure many of you who've pointed a camera at a very young child will know, it's not easy! To help with this, we've created production guides broken down into ages and stages. This means if a director is going to film a 0–3 month old, they should know what that child will likely be doing developmentally and they'll know the shots we're after.

It's not like they're following a script. Instead, they're looking for non-verbal signs of communication and they need to leave the camera there long enough to see them.

For each of those ages and stages we've also got our evidence-based key techniques, be it responding to the babble of a 6–9 month old, tuning into the interests of a 9–12 month old or following the lead of a 12–18 month old toddler. These are all things that the production companies we work with are keenly looking out for as they film with children.

The filming process

We found that filming with such young children and needing to get such specific shots meant that our processes became counterintuitive. Usually the cuts get faster and faster and you go where the action is. For our films we like to dwell on simple interactions so we can capture

the 'serve and return' between parent and child.

There's also fluidity to our shoots. There's no point trying to get a child to point and pop bubbles when they really want to play peekaboo! We have to adapt and spot good quality interactions between parent and child. By having a rapport with the production company and by being flexible, we always come away with something.

So what's it like being a camera operator on one of our films? Jake Cassels, MD of The Connected Set, says, "Any moment you have that feeling that a perfectly planned shoot will break into complete chaos – and it often does! For *Tiny Happy People*, the child you are filming with is in charge and that's the way it should be.

Photo: courtesy of BBC Education

Following their lead can result in some brilliant responses and some excellent resources as a result, but you need good humour and patience to pull it off."

Expert review

Before we share them on our website and on social media, the films are reviewed by experts. Depending on the topic, a midwife, health visitor, or early years professional and a speech & language therapist watches each film. They spot the 'gotchas' and ensure we reflect what's considered good practice on screen, whether that's demonstrating a good example of those key techniques to help children's language skills or ensuring babies are shown holding their own balance rather than in a walker.

The killer question we always ask is, "Would you recommend this film to a family you're working with?" If the answer is no, the film is re-edited until it passes the test!

Making a difference

Our aim is to increase a parent's understanding of language development in an accessible way. We show them how to boost their child's language skills through simple activities they can do at home. Our audience sees their lives reflected on screen and they see the opportunity to do the same activities with *their* child. And that, ultimately, is our aim.

If we can get parents to replicate what they're watching, and if they keep doing it, it will support language development in line with their child's potential. This in turn will help close the UK's word gap. And that's transformative.

Photos: courtesy of BBC Education

Lit in Colour: Creating Drama and Giving Voices to New Plays for Children Across the UK

Margaret Bartley, Editorial Director, Classics, Drama and Literary Studies at Bloomsbury Publishing

Theatre helps us to see a different perspective from our own. We're shown humanity, psychology, motivations, conflict and resolution. We as the audience get to witness the trajectory of individuals other than ourselves and, increasingly, it is representative of all people in our communities, all our cultures and backgrounds.

The teaching and studying of plays and texts in school moves at a slightly slower pace, driven by limited resources, teacher workloads and often lack of access to the right plays, texts and content. Many teachers are passionate about creating change. From conversations with the teaching community, we know that there is a desire to teach representative, exciting plays from modern writers of all backgrounds and races, but they often don't know what to teach or how to handle some of the difficult conversations that may arise from teaching these diverse texts.

We really welcome the changes the exam boards, schools and teachers are making to shape the curriculum and ensure young people are able to read, enjoy and study a range of work reflective of their experience and interests, but at Bloomsbury, we believe there is so much more we can do. This is where our partnership in the Lit in Colour initiative comes in.

In March of this year, Bloomsbury announced that it had joined forces with Penguin Random House and The Runnymede Trust's Lit in Colour campaign. Launched in 2020, Lit in Colour aims to support schools in diversifying the teaching of English and to increase students' access to texts by writers of colour and from minority ethnic backgrounds. Last year, their report found that less than 1% of GCSE students in England study a book by a writer of colour and we know from the exam board's specifications that this number is even less when looking at plays.

Bloomsbury's established play portfolio and playwright relationships will complement and expand on the current Lit in Colour initiative, widening the study of plays at GCSE, AS and A Level English. Under our Methuen Drama imprint, we will work with schools to introduce new plays that will create more representative and inclusive drama experiences within the English curriculum.

We are thrilled to have two Bloomsbury play texts and two Bloomsbury fiction books already selected to be set texts on the Pearson Lit in Colour Pioneers Programme – *The Empress* by Tanika Gupta and *Refugee Boy* by Benjamin Zephaniah, adapted for the stage by Lemn Sissay, *Home Fire* by Kamila Shamsie and *A Thousand Splendid Suns* by Khaled Hosseini. We are proudly supporting the Lit in Colour Pioneers programme by donating copies of these texts to the schools that have chosen to teach them, and will continue to work with the authors on providing valuable support and resources to teachers beginning to introduce these texts to the classroom.

We have started to put the foundations in place for our own programme. Publishing has its own ambitions and plans in the Diversity and Inclusion space and so for Lit in Colour, as a very first step, we have created our own Advisory Board, where some of the best and most influential people currently working in theatre can help drive the programme. mezze eade, Pooja Ghai and Tanika Gupta have all joined us to ensure that the developed programme meets the needs of teachers, represents new and exciting talent in the performance and drama space and makes the drama experience in schools the best it can be.

For those who are not aware of their backgrounds, mezze eade is currently Talent Development Manager at the Donmar Warehouse and an Education Associate at The Old Vic; Pooja Ghai is Artistic Director of Tamasha Theatre Company and is an award-winning director, actor, and mentor who is recognised as a fierce advocate for giving voice to marginalised groups; finally, playwright Tanika

Gupta MBE has written over 25 stage plays that have been produced in major theatres across the UK and has written regularly for Radio and Television drama. Winning numerous awards for her work, she has been writer in residence at the National Theatre and Soho Theatre.

How will this benefit the education community?

Our involvement in the Lit in Colour campaign focuses on supporting teachers and students in the classroom. The Advisory Board will guide the development of an '(incomplete) Lit in Colour list' of plays by authors of colour that we will make available to all teachers who would like to be part of our programme.

We will then be arranging teacher webinar sessions in collaboration with Lit in Colour to increase and focus on the awareness of these plays by diverse playwrights and promote the '(incomplete) Lit in Colour list' of plays, introducing more options for teachers to choose from.

We will also be developing and supporting a series of educational resources on selected plays, partnering with playwrights and theatres, for use in the classroom. These resources will include playwright Q&A webinars, videos, discussion questions, and a focus on performance. As well as support for teaching some plays that teachers may find tricky or challenging.

We want to make sure that the programme we develop incorporates as many views as possible. So, we are proud to be collaborating with the National Theatre and Open Drama UK to conduct our own research, with the aim of capturing as many teacher voices as we can to help us better understand how to bring about genuine change to the way English Literature is taught in schools. We want to expand the curriculum to include new voices and new cultures and, for some schools, a new way of thinking about literature.

Our aim is to support those who teach drama or play texts with a complete package and to make the whole experience of plays and literature fun and engaging and relevant for children from all backgrounds.

Studying play texts can be hugely rewarding for students of both Drama and English Literature. Plays dynamically tell stories and give voices to a wide range of characters like no other literary texts, reflecting and enhancing the lives of all students, empowering them to find their own voices and identities. Working in partnership with the theatre and education communities, we want to ensure students have the opportunity to encounter and engage with texts by writers of colour and from diverse backgrounds, reflective of the rich breadth of our society and the many cultures it consists of. Studying drama texts in particular can offer students new ways to express themselves creatively, building confidence and mutual understanding in the classroom, on the stage and in the world beyond it.

The passion for the teaching and learning of English Literature in Britain's classrooms has shone through in the Lit in Colour programme. True diversity in education cannot be achieved by one entity alone, so the more we work together and collaborate the more impact and rapid change we can bring about.

Our vibrant fiction and new playwriting lists offer myriad titles to increase the choice of texts, reflecting the diverse and inclusive society from which, and for which, they are written. I smile as I write this, because I know that Bloomsbury can be part of the change that we would all like to see in the teaching of drama in education and look forward to playing our part in inspiring new generations of readers and playwrights through Lit in Colour.

Find out more about the project and how you can get involved, at www.Bloomsbury.com/LitinColour.

Photo: by Hamish Kale on Unsplash

Where We Stand on Diversity and Inclusivity: A Discussion

Mel Rodrigues, CEO, Gritty Talent and **Jessica Schibli**, Head of Diversity & Inclusion, BBC Children's & Education

*The **Children's Media Yearbook** asked Mel Rodrigues and Jessica Schibli to take a temperature check on diversity and inclusion within our field and discuss what work needs doing ahead.*

Mel: I'm the founder and CEO of Gritty Talent, which is a talent and technology company specifically working to introduce people from underrepresented groups into, on and off screen roles, via tech and via mentoring and nurturing. My background, for the best part of 20 years, is in current affairs and factual, and I did a bit of Children's for BBC Learning. And my most recent role, that I've just finished, has been as a creative diversity lead at Channel 4, specifically looking at ethnic diversity in terms of talent, and also working with diverse led indies to try to tip the balance as to where money goes when it comes to the indie landscape.

Jessica: I'm the Head of Diversity and Inclusion for BBC Children's & Education. My role is quite vast – looking after workforce diversity as well as creative diversity – ensuring representation in our staff base and our content. For our internal staff and leadership teams we have targets around gender, ethnicity, disability, and we're also now monitoring and introducing targets for socioeconomic diversity. We've led a series of initiatives addressing the culture of BBC Children's & Education – building a sense of inclusion and an environment that fosters belonging and full participation from all – especially key as we bring more diversity to our workforce. We're also committed to ensuring that the production teams making our content reflect our audience to create high quality, representative and authentic content for children.

As a public service broadcaster, we take a great deal of pride in our unique position to serve our audience, with an acute sense of duty and responsibility to all children regardless of who they are and where they are from. Representation is important for all audiences, but it's even more so for children – we cannot underestimate the impact of young people seeing themselves reflected on-screen. I feel passionately about the role that media can play in showing children that everyone is welcome and that anyone can be anything – away from the unconscious biases that we often hold as adults. I love that our current content seamlessly integrates a black female firefighter or a family with two dads or an autistic race car driver. From my own personal experience, as someone who grew up watching BBC Children's TV broadcast from the broom-cupboard every day after school, I recall that it was quite 'normal' not to see anyone like me on-screen. But I remember it being actively noticed and remarked upon by my family and I when we did see someone from an Indian background – it was Krishnan Guru-Murthy presenting *Newsround* – there was a pleasant sense of surprise that: "Oh! Somebody that's from the same background as me."

Photo: by Sharon McCutcheon on Unsplash

And similarly years later, when Konnie Huq joined *Blue Peter* there was that same sense of acknowledgement and excitement.

Research clearly shows that media has a significant effect on how children feel about themselves and others, it can influence the difference between pride or insecurity in your identity, whether that relates to ethnicity, disability or socioeconomic status. Media can impact the way children see the world and how they interact with it, hopefully working towards building a more inclusive society for future generations.

Whilst there has been much progress in recent years to include representation on screen, and at BBC Children's & Education we are actively monitoring data to ensure that we are representing all aspects of diversity, the conversation is now turning more to authenticity. We acknowledge that it's not enough just to tick a box: we've got somebody with a disability, we've got somebody from a minority ethnic background; it's about making sure that those characters and that portrayal is authentic, and that will truly happen when the people writing the scripts, the people that are producing the programs, also have that lived experience.

Mel: What you said there is so true and the thing about representation and diversity that we're now moving hopefully away from is the tick-box attitude. "I have an Asian person, I have a disabled person; therefore I've ticked my boxes." It's really dangerous for people to think of diversity as a series of targets that you have to attain without being meaningfully interwoven into your editorial ambition, and how you view society –

and all the creative skill and talent that can come from lots of different people when you put them into a creative process.

We are moving away from this tick-box culture, but for a long time it just felt very difficult, and black stories, disabled stories have been treated as niche. I've worked with lots of talent who are fantastic, gifted presenters and experts, but happen to be in a wheelchair and they will be given a gig telling a disabled story. But why can't they be just as brilliant telling us that consumer story, or a food story, if they have those skills. So it's about people looking beyond the label and seeing creative skill.

The other side of it is about upcoming emerging talent having the aspirations to work in the creative sector. A lot of the stats we see about our industry say that it is still a very privileged workplace in the sense that the majority of people, particularly in mid to senior level roles are university educated, have parents that went to university. A higher proportion of the workforce in TV are privately educated and tend to live in the south of the UK. So the problem that we are trying to unpick as a sector now is if, behind camera, you are only represented by a relatively narrow band of society, how do you know you're telling the story right. And how do you know you can get authenticity right. And we've seen examples where stories have been told really wrong, because people have made assumptions and brought biases to storytelling that has meant that marginalised groups have been stereotyped or labelled in certain ways. I will be so chuffed the day that I turn on the TV and it's utterly unremarkable that a Muslim woman in a wheelchair is talking about DIY. At the moment it would be a thing. We've done

tick-boxing, but the drive now is towards it being woven into the fabric of our industry.

Jessica: In the last year, to really put intention into action, we supersized and expanded the scope of our BBC Children's & Education Diversity Fund to support off-screen diversity. It's open to a range of roles – we're supporting people joining the industry at entry level, but also in their mid-career progression. The Fund is specifically for people that are underrepresented in our industry in specific areas and roles. For example, we had an application for animation and for VFX, where data shows that gender is significantly underrepresented. So we've been able to fund and support more women in those roles. We also know as an industry that disability is hugely underrepresented, yet we're trying to tell those stories authentically on-screen – in the past year we have been able to support several talented disabled individuals in a range of roles from director to shooting AP, who have gone on to secure their next role in line with their career goals following their funded placement. We also have examples of individuals from low socioeconomic backgrounds and ethnic backgrounds who have been supported by the fund to take their next step in their career progression.

We've spent quite a bit of time reviewing and taking action to completely open up our recruitment process, especially as we know that we all have our own unconscious biases, which can come into effect especially when under stress or time pressures. To mitigate the effects of possible individual biases, we've introduced a framework to ensure our recruitment is more inclusive. Otherwise we'll just keep recruiting the same people that we've always recruited before. There's a lot to unpick there.

Mel: It's interesting, isn't it, particularly in the recruitment side of things. Inclusive recruitment is harder to do, and it takes more time. It involves people having to undo all the old habits, going to your black-book of who you know because you've got a quick turnaround and people you can rely on, and instead looking at talent who are not already networked into Children's TV. It's getting better, but some jobs still don't get advertised. And if they are advertised, where are they advertised? How inclusive is the wording? So there's all these things that we need to relearn.

Jessica: Across the industry there is often still a sense that when you're recruiting somebody from an underrepresented background or protected characteristic that you're taking a risk, it shows sometimes in the language we end up using: "We can't take a risk with this role because it's really important." Across the industry we will need to work to undo some of our old ways of thinking – to be open and truly buy in to the benefits of having a range of diverse voices and different people around the table to create the best content that we can for our audiences.

Mel: It's interesting what you say about taking risks and the perception of risk. One of the projects we did at Gritty was working with the team who make *JoJo and Gran Gran*, A Productions, based in Bristol. And they wanted to do a really big analysis of what's worked and what's not worked for them and the conclusion was: this is hard graft, it takes years. The results they saw for series 2 and 3 were because of seeds they had sown two years earlier for series 1. So one of the biggest messages has to be that you cannot just write a Diversity and Inclusion (D&I) policy and put some adverts out and expect the problem to be solved.

There is this long road, and there's incremental gains each time, and you have to be alert to what's working, and what's not. People can say: "Well, you know, I did an inclusive advert and that's that." But has it worked? How many more people from different groups did apply? Did you get feedback from them? What was their feedback on the recruitment process?

What we now need to do isn't the glamorous work. It's not the big headlines work, about multimillion-pound pots of money. It's the forensic work on what do we think works over here. And if it's not working, let's not do that and let's try something else instead. So it's slow gains, but I think from the *JoJo and Gran Gran* case study, we learned that creating a really inclusive and diverse pipeline is possible, but it requires investments of time and money and patience, and admitting that not every new talent we bring on is going to work. There's a huge pressure you put on that person from an underrepresented group to succeed. It may not be for them, and that's okay.

Jessica: I know we talked earlier about how we don't want to be ticking boxes, but I think it's also important to acknowledge that to progress with our D&I ambitions, we do need to have targets, we do need to have data. We can't measure inclusion, and plot it easily on a graph, in the same way we can for workforce diversity, but for every initiative and goal, it's important to articulate and report on success criteria. We've done this initiative: what's the impact, what's the benefit? How do we tweak it? And how do we keep making it better? This has helped us at BBC Children's & Education monitor our progress and highlight where we need to focus our efforts.

Ultimately it's about having that representation in the production teams, in the writers' rooms, and actually doing it right at the beginning of the process – making sure that at the pitch meetings, we are having those conversations. So, who's going to be in the team? What's the production leadership going to be like? Have we got diversity and lived experience in influential roles off-screen?

Mel: I would like to see the industry look more at things like allyship. How people can support others, who are underrepresented every day, through the way they behave. And so it's about the culture of teams, people understanding what being a good ally is. A really important part of what we touched on is intersectionality and socioeconomic groups. We as a sector are only beginning to understand these things. Socioeconomic background is going to be one of the biggest areas that we are going to unpick in terms of the equity of which people have to access which jobs. We haven't looked at it as much as we have looked at things like disability and race. If you think about Children's, you want children around the UK to see their parents, friends, aunties, uncles, cousins going off to work in creative jobs – and at the moment we have a real problem, depending on where you are in the UK, and whether or not you have access to higher education really determines what type of industry you go into. It's that: "If you can't see it, you can't be it." If you've never seen someone working in animation, you don't know that you can make an amazing kids' animation. If you're not seeing someone work on a kid's drama, you don't know you can do it too. So I think off-screen, socioeconomic mobility is going to be a really big issue. To make sure that off-screen we're as representative as we are on-screen.

Photo: by IIONA VIRGIN on Unsplash

Photo: by Jonathan Borba on Unsplash

Photo: by Artem Kniaz on Unsplash

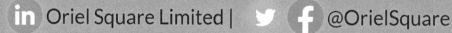

A Sustainable Future:
On and Behind the Screen

Genevieve Margrett, Communications Manager, albert

In 2019, a study was undertaken in Uganda to explore the impact that a strong role model on screen could have on the attitudes and actions of a group of schoolchildren[1]. The children were asked to watch *The Queen of Katwe* – a film that tells the true story of Phiona Mutsei, a young girl who went from living in poverty in the slums of Kampala to playing chess at an international level. The results were notable; concluding that "watching a role model in the form of a movie, positively impacted students' exam performance, particularly of female students, and had positive effects on their continuation in education."

This example is just one of many that illustrate the positive impact that on-screen stories can have on real world challenges. The stories we consume help to shape us. They can educate and inspire, providing us with an alternative view point and a different outlook on life. And while this can apply to any age group, it's arguably within children's media that the greatest impact lies – where an enthusiastic and willing audience is ready to be transported by a story and believe in the seemingly impossible.

For many, the 'seemingly impossible' challenge of the moment is the climate crisis. When

the UN calls for "rapid, far reaching and unprecedented changes in all aspects of society," it is easy to question *how* this might be achieved. For the past decade, albert – the leading screen industry organisation for environmental sustainability – has been supporting the film and TV industry to reduce the environmental impacts of production and to create content that supports a vision for a sustainable future.

It's an organisation that many in the children's industry have backed since its inception; some of the first productions to use albert's production carbon calculator were children's shows and when we launched our *planet placement* resource the children's industry was already putting it into practice with shows like *Thomas and Friends*, weaving five of the UNs sustainability goals (Quality Education, Gender Equality, Sustainable Cities and Communities, Responsible Consumption and Production, and Life on Land) into its storylines.

Like albert, the children's industry realised that whilst the work we do behind the scenes to reduce our environmental impact remains hugely important on the road to Net Zero, it's the stories we tell on-screen that will ultimately have the

---

[1] https://mbrg.bsg.ox.ac.uk/mind-and-behaviour-projects/going-movies-can-help-you-school-impact-queen-katwe-students

biggest impact. We can't pass the responsibility of tackling change onto a generation which didn't cause it. We must do all we can to tackle the issue head on, but sadly this is still likely to be a crisis young people will inherit. So helping them to understand the issues and build resilience, showing them the potential routes forward, as well as optimism for their own futures is key. And the window of opportunity to do this is small.

A recent survey by IPSOS and Futerra[2] found "surprisingly high levels of fatalism concerning climate change among young people [under 35s] and a new inequality of attitude dependent on age, wealth and location." This rather alarming headline suggests that helping children navigate and understand the issues surrounding climate change at a young age is key to our collective global success at combating the climate crisis. Furthermore, when you consider research that shows children may be their parents' best climate change teachers[3] – the potential for children to change the world is truly unrivalled.

At COP26 in Glasgow in 2021, albert launched its Climate Content Pledge with 12 leading broadcasters and streamers being the first signatories. The pledge was a rallying cry to the global industry to do more – and better – climate storytelling on-screen across all genres. Time will tell how each of the broadcasters puts this pledge into action but no doubt children's programming will play an integral role – because if anyone can authentically bring climate storylines into their content using humour, pathos and ultimately inspiring change, it's those who work to create world class content for young people.

Back in the 90s, when climate change was mostly considered an outlier topic barely worth worrying about, let alone covering in mainstream media, children were watching *Captain Planet and the Planeteers* and learning about the importance of the natural world through a team of superheroes. It's a cartoon with the tagline 'The Power is Yours!' that inspired Ghanian-Canadian animator Gyimah Gariba to create the CBC series *Big Blue* – which introduces climate change to a young audience.

Perhaps it was also shows like Captain Planet that inspired the teams behind current climate-focussed shows like Sky Original *Obki,* C5's *Go Green with the Grimwades* or CBBC's *Planet Defenders* – and who knows in turn which climate champions of the future these shows are currently inspiring.

As David Attenborough succinctly put it when he posted on Instagram – "Saving our planet is now a communications challenge." It's our industry that has a unique opportunity to tell stories that can explore alternative low carbon futures and help audiences to imagine and believe in a sustainable way of living. Let the children's TV industry carry on as it often has in this space, leading the way, highlighting best practice and educating the next generation.

Obki. Sky Original. Produced by Obki Productions and made by Ritzy Animation. All Sky Originals in the UK, since 2019, have been Carbon Neutral, and produced in line with their Sustainable Production Principles and albert certificated

[2] https://www.ipsos.com/en-uk/climate-fatalism-grips-young-people-worldwide-while-urgency-solution-oriented-media-grows

[3] https://www.scientificamerican.com/article/children-change-their-parents-minds-about-climate-change/

Sustainability Case Study:
JoJo & Gran Gran

Andrew Snowdon, Production Manager, BBC Studios Kids & Family

JoJo & Gran Gran is a mixed-media series made by BBC Studios Kids & Family, which combines animation with live-action elements. Set in London, 4 year old 'JoJo' and her wise Grandmother 'Gran Gran' walk hand-in-hand as they explore their local community – visiting places and enjoying activities that we hope our young audience may also like to do in their own lives. At BBC Studios we are always extremely conscious of the impact our content can have on a child's life and the responsibility we carry to educate our audience in taking care of the world in which we all live.

On the animation side of *JoJo & Gran Gran*, we work hard to include environmental practices in the everyday lives of our characters – when Gran Gran walks with JoJo to the local shop, they will pass houses bedecked in solar panels, carry their own reusable bags to collect their groceries and drop their waste into the correct recycle bin.

They might wave at their neighbour Cynthia as she tends to her garden or join JoJo's friends as they eat a picnic out of reusable Tupperware in the community garden. These examples of sustainable living were deeply rooted in our production team's minds when *JoJo & Gran*

Gran's animated world was being created and is a key part of our Assistant Script Editor's job to make sustainability suggestions to weave into each script. These design additions to our series are sometimes added at extra cost to ensure that they are noticeable to our viewers.

Images: courtesy of BBC Children's In-House Productions / A Productions

In the live-action elements of *JoJo & Gran Gran* we invite local children to try some of the activities that are performed in the animation.

This allows us to show our young audience that they too can experience in real life what *JoJo & Gran Gran* enjoy in their animated world. Once again, sustainable practices are at the forefront of the ideas for these VTs and woven-in to the stories that we tell. In a recently televised episode, a young boy learned all about how to look after the insects in our garden by building a 'bug hotel' out of recyclable materials, whilst in an episode about Pond Dipping, two children are taught about the importance of wildlife in our natural world, even in urban areas.

Behind-the-camera, the BBC have made a commitment to be 'Net Zero by 2030' and we are challenged at the Greenlight stage of our productions to think about how we can become more environmentally-friendly. At the beginning of our production, we sent a 'Green Memo' to all of our partners and employees that documented a series of sustainable goals we wanted to work towards – this included simple actions like using Zoom instead of travelling where possible, working with catering suppliers that do not use single-use plastics and looking to reuse props & background decorations as much as we can.

As a BBC Studios Kids & Family production we fully acknowledge our responsibility to not only be a sustainable production ourselves, but to educate our young viewers about the necessity to look after the beautiful world around us. Through *JoJo & Gran Gran*, we have a unique opportunity to do this that we continually strive to build-upon.

Sustainability Case Study: **Sol**

Gráinne McGuinness, Creative Director, Paper Owl Films
and **Gavin Halpin**, Managing Director, Paper Owl Films

Sol, produced by Paper Owl Films, is an ambitious animated film that was the result of the passion, talent and love of a collective of creatives, broadcasters and funding bodies dedicated to doing justice to a delicate story. The 28 minute film follows little boy Sol after his whole world is plunged into darkness when his beloved grandmother – his Nonee – dies. Moving like a shadow through his days, he reluctantly becomes the only person who can bring the light back into the world before it is lost forever. He journeys through a subconscious landscape made from the keepsakes and memories of his Nonee's photo album. This breath-taking animated landscape is as rich, layered and beautiful as the life Nonee led. But it is also a place crumbling into decay, and it takes all of Sol's strength and courage to journey through this confusing land to beat the darkness.

Sol was created in CelAction, with AfterEffects used to create the atmosphere of Sol's quest. Developing this world took a lot of thought and creativity; this is the subconscious land of Nonee's lifetime from the perspective of a 12 year old boy. In *Sol,* grief speaks a visual language, a language carefully woven into an unforgettable visual world that is as richly layered and complex as Sol's grief. *Sol* is an absorbing emotional quest that shows how to powerfully address difficult subjects for young audiences – if we have commissioners who are willing to run with risky content.

Images: courtesy of Paper Owl Films

Children live in the real world – that of pain, death, struggle and difficulty – they deserve to be positively represented on screen. *Sol* proves that not only can this be done, but when done well it will attract audiences at home and in the international marketplace. *Sol* was a unique collaboration between the Celtic broadcasters on these islands: TG4, S4C, BBC Alba, with funding from NI Screen's ILBF and Screen fund, the BFI's

YACF and our distributor Aardman. Produced in our indigenous languages and bringing the voices of the Celtic regions into the mainstream was a beautiful celebration of the diversity of our shared experience.

Even with a difficult subject matter, hugely ambitious creative and a surprise lockdown pipeline, we ended up with a pan broadcaster event on the 21st December which saw CiTV, ITV Hub, All4 and My5 all broadcast the film on the Winter Solstice to mark a moment of light on the longest night of the year. In a landscape of disruption and uncertainty, *Sol* received huge praise for its beauty and power on the longest night of the year. A unique broadcast in a unique year subsequently made for a unique broadcast event!

When *Sol,* designed to help children with grief, was greenlit at the end of 2019, we could never have known the poignant relevance it would have for audiences in 2020. And we could not have predicted the challenges of moving an entire pipeline to remote working.

Sustainability was at the heart of *Sol* from the beginning, with albert Certification part of our funding agreement – and having albert as a structure and process was invaluable. Prior to producing *Sol*, Paper Owl had already engaged with the spirit of albert, attending information sessions and training. It was a logical step for our company to incorporate the guidelines and green philosophy promoted by the initiative into our standard production practices.

Key players on the production team were given overall responsibility for keeping the team on track for their sustainability goals. This was key

Images: courtesy of Paper Owl Films

to making sure that when things got busy, we didn't lose sight of our goals. Then assigning this responsibility to a junior member was great for their morale, and shared initiatives like this are positive for the whole team – everyone felt like they were contributing.

Editorially, *Sol* highlights the beauty, wisdom and age of our world – apple trees, blue skies, the earth and soil. We used textures and the physicality of memories through photographs and scrapbooks, for example leaf pressings, to subtly weave in the themes around respect for the planet and each other. *Sol* incorporates ideas around the shared Celtic languages and wisdom implicit to the British Isles and, within that, the idea of our shared experiences on the earth and the need to protect and look after it. It is a message about the permanence of what we bring to the earth, the love we leave behind and the energy that carries on long after our physical impact has ceased. So being kind to the earth and producing in the most positive way possible on all levels was really important.

albert's production training provided a good starting point for the core team members, highlighting lots of opportunities for practical ways to reduce impact. The production process began with a Green Memo, sent to the entire production team, outlining *Sol*'s intentions to be an albert certified production and explaining how the team were going to achieve it.

Using albert's Carbon Calculator, the production team calculated that 85% of their carbon footprint would be produced from the office and presented some 'Office Green Goals' in the Green Memo to help address this. Goals included:

- Turning off lights and keeping desk lamp use to a minimum, using natural light when possible
- Opening windows rather than turning on fans during the heat
- Closing doors rather than turning on the heating when it was cold
- Shutdown of equipment, lights and closing of doors after hours
- Removal of water coolers from the animation and sound studios
- Keeping a smaller fridge in the kitchen and limiting use of the dishwasher to once a day
- Meat free Mondays.

The pandemic changed everything, of course, and we found working remotely did have environmental benefits – less travel, less commuting, in fact the entire project was produced during the lockdown. Our carbon footprint and final project calculations reduced dramatically. It was positive in an otherwise very challenging time.

Taking charge

Sol was a unique production created in unique circumstances. It dealt with grief. It brought the culture and voices of our Celtic regions to the fore. It drew together a unique broadcaster and funder model – and was a successful example of production completed during testing times. Perhaps more significantly it was a role model for both the editorial and production side of engaging with albert's sustainability initiatives. As Gavin Halpin, Managing Director of Paper Owl Films concluded:

"It does take the entire team to buy in for something like this – there's little to be gained on sustainable initiatives if you don't go 100% in. Our case study wasn't one of hardship – our sustainability practices just had to be very well organised."

Can We Help Our Children Save the Planet?

Gary Pope, CEO of KI and Children's Ambassador for Products of Change

We're in trouble. All of us. In fact, unless we halve our carbon emissions by 2025, irreparable damage will be done. Actually, it's not all of us, is it? It's just those of us that will be around in 50 years time. Like, well, our children and our grandchildren.

On April 4th this year the Intergovernmental Panel on Climate Change (IPCC) report was released. And in it a glimmer, a slither, of hope that we might just be able to get all of this climate change back in its box and, if we hit some pretty robust targets by 2030, we could prevent a global climate increase of 1.5°C, and ensure at least some semblance of a future for our planet. But radical action is needed and it is needed from today. Now. Not tomorrow. Now. Or as they say in South Africa, NOW NOW.

The report makes it very clear that by doing the right thing – in fact the only thing – and adapting our lifestyles and behaviours, then we can make happen a 40–70% reduction in greenhouse gas emissions by 2050 and that might just be enough to save the future. Maybe.

Thing is, limiting warming to 1.5°C (2.7°F) needs greenhouse gas emissions to peak before 2025 and be reduced by 43% by 2030. Simultaneously, methane would also need to be reduced by about 30%. Reality is that this is not going to happen. We will exceed this temperature threshold. BUT we might just be able to get it back down again by the end of the century... if we get our acts together.

So what am I writing about this in the Children's Media Yearbook for? I wear two hats. One is as CEO of KI. That's my day job. But it's my side hustle that I have suddenly realised is the most important one. I am the Children's Ambassador for Products of Change and my role is to act as an advocate for children through the work the group does. Right now, children need a bit of advocacy. One of the many wonderful things about our industry is that we genuinely care about the people we make stuff for. And I am asking you to really double down on that care.

In our game we don't think of ourselves as particularly polluting, do we? Our computers might use a bit of electricity and we might have to catch a flight to Kidscreen or MIP, but we don't sit in huge factories chuffing out all manner of planet choking toxicity, do we? No, we don't. But our model very often needs consumer products to make it work. And as an industry, consumer products uses a vast amount of energy and emits mind boggling quantities of carbon... supply chain, manufacturing, shipping and delivery. You get the idea. Sure, there is some fantastic work being done by LEGO and Mattel, to name just two, but how many people realistically get their consumer products programme away with the really big boys, who have their sustainability action plans in place and are leading the way? No, most of us never see our product in the showroom of a behemoth with strong and necessary corporate governance. But the world is changing and as the saying goes, we need to be the change we want to see. There are many, many companies out there that are being the change. Amazing firms are designing, manufacturing and delivering great products that families love without upsetting Mother Nature. So the first thing I am asking you to do, as you think about how your next big hit comes to market, is to consider choosing partners that are being the change the planet needs and that children deserve.

But it is in the characters we develop and in the stories that we tell where even more value can be found. Between the ages of 5 and 7, that wonderful, very real period of childhood, life-long behaviours are formed. We are of course, educators as well as storytellers.

Children know that there's a problem with the planet but they don't know what it really means to make the changes that are necessary.

> **41% of children across the UK and US do not think that the efforts they make can make a difference to climate change, but they still want to do something about it.**

We have a responsibility to give that ambition hope. They need to know that they can make a difference. 93% of UK and US children are doing something every day to take action against climate change. We have the opportunity to amplify this action.

Children look to the stories that we create to understand the world around them. They identify with characters and are inspired by them. They model their behaviour on them and they pretend to be them with their friends as they play. And if play is the work of the child, then this is important work to be doing.

The UN Sustainable Development Goals offer us all a framework on which to build the future for our children. There are 17 of them and they are designed to enable all of us to do something.

Photo: by Alan Rodriguez on Unsplash

The fourth Sustainable Development Goal (SDG) is: *Quality Education*. The work we do educates and the media at our disposal, not just broadcast, YouTube and Netflix, but TikTok and whatever is materialising in the Metaverse, all point to the growing demand on content to have some educational value. But I don't mean letters and numbers. It's attitudes and behaviours that we can help develop too. Everything a child consumes contributes to their world view. We have a responsibility to contribute everything we can to support the delivery of SDG 4. The UN's stated aim for this goal is that every child has the opportunity to have free primary and secondary education by 2030. It's baffling to me that this is even a goal. A billionaire can offer the GDP of a nation to purchase a social media plaything and yet there are, and will remain, kids that can't read and write. Most of our kids can read and write and so in the spirit of SDG 4, what can we do through the tools of our trade to give our kids Quality Education and help them do their bit to save the planet?

The work that Products of Change does as a membership organisation is designed to support, encourage and perpetuate companies and brands in meeting their sustainability goals through education that informs change. We are here to help you ensure that what you create for children positively impacts their future. Socrates said "The secret of change is to focus all of your energy, not on fighting the old, but on building the new." Why not become a member of Products of Change and use the tools we've built for you there, to help focus energy on saving this beautiful blue planet?

Photo: by Callum Shaw on Unsplash

Photo: by Margot RICHARD on Unsplash

Virtual Production – Entertainment that's Virtual and Green

Peter Stanley-Ward, Director, Treehouse Digital

Virtual Production (VP) is changing high-end media content production. Combining digital video production with VFX/CGI, game-engines (e.g. Unity and Unreal Engine) and virtual/augmented reality technologies, VP enables new ways of making film and TV, from initiation to delivery. Exemplified in real-time, on-set visual effects on high-end drama productions such as *The Mandalorian* and in many ways an inheritor of long evolving virtual studio approaches, VP approaches, and possibilities, are having an impact on core disciplines within film and television, including development, production design, set design, cinematography, VFX, animation, directing and beyond. As yet, however, VP hasn't made a significant impact in children's media, but Treehouse Digital are throwing everything at experimenting with and applying VP in ways that are bringing the techniques and practices into the children's production landscape.

From Day One at Treehouse it was our aim to create a 'one stop factory' where we could build our own world and characters and provide high quality entertainment. We've been on this journey for some time and have tried many paths to realise this dream, but it was when we saw Epic Games' Virtual Production demo that we knew we had found the missing piece. VP was the answer and we wasted no time diving straight in... In two months, we gatecrashed conferences so that in between keynotes we could run on stage and quickly throw a camera on the LED screens on display. We downloaded the Unreal Engine and locked one of us in a room to learn the basics. We cold-called a local LED screen company so that we could see an Unreal scene on their screens… and our enthusiasm didn't go unnoticed. In the few months that followed we received a MegaGrant from Epic Games to continue our journey to using VP on an Indie level. Fast-forward just two years from that and we now have our own VP studio in Bournemouth and have worked with Netflix, Amazon Studios, BBC and others – providing a VP service.

We have been creating short form entertainment for seven years and we are really proud to have completed our first short film made entirely in Unreal Engine and continue to refine our craft and partner with artists on our journey.

This is a moment in time when a new way of working with technology has enabled the creation of incredible visual entertainment. You find the right talented people, create the right conditions and the pipeline is ready to go. One thing we hadn't foreseen, however, was how making entertainment through VP has a future that could be completely green.

> "a goal of providing entertainment with zero emissions and very low carbon footprint is a very real possibility"

Last year Treehouse invested in a small fleet of electric cars for the staff. Our studio is located on a hillside by the coast and is one of the sunniest places in the UK. It didn't take long for us to do the maths and see a future, not far away, where we could power our studio with solar and wind. Then, combine that with the capability to create high quality images with a modest number of artists and it becomes clear that a goal of providing entertainment with zero emissions and very low carbon footprint is a very real possibility.

Our next step is to partner with a platform that can support us in creating entire shows and movies all within a warehouse on the south coast of the UK. And to do so 'completely green'. We're already developing the material, refining the art and implementing the solar and wind power to do it.

Case Study: Paradise Hacked

In 2021 we began developing a series with the BFI's Young Audience Content Fund. The way in which we want to make the show is part of its unique appeal. We are proposing to use both LED live action elements and complete CG animation. Whilst we began developing this IP we also began to build our own studio. *Paradise Hacked* is a large-scale, sci-fi fantasy that has high production value. A show like this would normally take up many locations and studio space; however, it soon became very clear to

us that by employing VP techniques the show could realistically be made entirely in our studio. We also have the added advantage that at Treehouse we are developing and writing the show as well as bringing it to life – so the idea starts at the Treehouse and we're able to plan the shoot whilst the idea continues to develop. For us this is the future of entertainment. Not only does it give us independence as artists, but it also allows us to refine the craft of storytelling in a controlled environment that's completely sustainable.

Photo: courtesy of Treehouse Digital

dubit

· · · · · · · · ·

EXPERIENCE THE METAVERSE

Dubit makes games for the metaverse, kids and for eSports. Founded in 1999, we have over 20 years experience of researching and creating digital gaming worlds and experiences for global businesses and innovative startups.

With offices in the UK and US, our team of 100 professionals designs and develops massively interactive live events for the metaverse, in Roblox, Minecraft and Core.

DIGITAL | RESEARCH | MARKETING

www.dubitlimited.com

Let's Go Live – During a Pandemic

Maddie Moate, CBeebies and CBBC Presenter, YouTube Creator, Author and Podcaster and
Greg Foot, Science Journalist on BBC Radio 4, Podcast Producer and Presenter and Event Host

Co-hosts of popular YouTube live family science show Let's Go Live, Maddie and Greg, talk us through their experiences of pulling together a successful live show during lockdown.

Maddie: OK, Greg. What's your name? What do you do?

Greg: Um, hi, I'm Greg. I'm a scientist by training, now a science presenter and a producer of… goodness am I listing these?

Maddie: Yes.

Greg: YouTube and TV and podcasts and radio and on-stage shows – and theatre now, because we've got our theatre tour.

Maddie: It's fair to say we always feel really awkward when somebody asks us what we do, because the answer is we wear many different hats.

Greg: But it is useful that we wore all those hats, in order to make *Let's Go Live* happen. What about you Maddie? What do you do?

Maddie: Well, my name is Maddie. I am a children's television presenter. Perhaps best known for some of my work on CBeebies, including presenting a show called *Maddie's Do You Know?*

Greg: And she got a BAFTA for that, by the way.

Maddie: Cheers. It was a while back, but I'll take that. And aside from TV, I've been working on various YouTube channels, including my own YouTube content. I'm also a podcaster and an author. And occasionally I do stage shows and dress up as things like lobsters and trees and mice and old women called Beryl. I get all the best parts!

Greg: So let's talk about *Let's Go Live* in lockdown.

Maddie: We should go back to what was the beginning of March 2020.

Greg: Just over two years ago… When lockdown was looming, we realised that there were going to be a lot of kids off school and families facing the prospect of home-schooling for the first time.

Maddie: We realised that that was an opportunity for us to help: a way that we could give back. Having both been content creators – Greg being a professional science communicator for many years, and myself having worked in this field making videos for children for a while – we were in a really good position to start making online science content to help with science home-schooling.

Greg: We started on day one of lockdown. The initial idea was just to open up a laptop and talk to the lens. But then I got excited about a bit of software I found called Ecamm that allowed me to do live vision mixing, so I spent the weekend plugging in our old DSLR cameras. I could plug them all in and essentially set up a live studio. Then I got excited about branding, so we had proper logos. This was all done over the weekend – a really crazy, bonkers, but fun weekend.

Maddie: We went live at 11am on Monday 23rd of March with a show that was the two of us, in our spare room, sat at a desk, looking at one main camera. Did we have a second camera then? I think we did. A desk cam.

Greg: We also had a bird cam! Pointing out of the window at the bird feeders. We started with a branded hold screen, a countdown on the screen and some music, and then up we came. "Hello, everyone!"

"I'm Greg."

"I'm Maddie and…"

"WE ARE LIVE!"

That became our catchphrase that kids would shout at the screen!

Maddie: We realised early on that the show would be more successful if we could become those reliable, trusted faces that could give parents a break at the same time every single day. So from day one, we decided to go live at 11am, Monday to Friday, for as long as we needed to.

Greg: There's a lot of live chat involved in the shows and we'd be asking the kids and the families questions… there was a big interactive quiz… and a make, a craft, or a science experiment.

Maddie: Yes it was a quiz and activities, games or experiments, depending on what we could find or what we could create or make up that best fitted with the week's theme and topic.

Greg: You're probably now wondering "How did you prep a 30+ minute interactive live show everyday?" Well, we didn't do anything else. It was a silver-lining of the situation, to focus on one thing, and our one thing was spending 17 hours every day, Monday to Sunday, coming up with exciting ideas for quizzes and games and experiments. Very quickly, we started going out and filming little videos too, editing them in the afternoon to drop in as VTs into the shows.

Maddie: We had to start doing that because there's only so much you can do inside a very small spare room and we are naturally quite ambitious. During space week, we decided to design different types of parachutes to slow down an egg drop. It's a classic science experiment, except it was Easter time, so we made them chocolate eggs, and it was for our Mars Landing special episode. But we couldn't do that within the spare room, so the afternoon before, we filmed a VT, edited it that night, and then we dropped the VT into the live show.

Greg: The user generated content was a big aspect of building such a great audience, too. Families would try the experiments in the afternoon and then send us an email with pics or a video. We got kids of all different ages doing this stuff together with parents and guardians. And that became a big part of the show.

Maddie: It was seeing their contributions that actually helped us realise the gap we were filling. We were creating family content that was silly and visual enough for little ones to enjoy but, equally, was pushing the science and education up to Key Stage 2, even Key Stage 3 for the older ones. We made sure that it was interactive, there was an element of competition, but always in a fun, friendly way.

Greg: A great example is 'bounce pads' where you take some cans, like a baked bean can, and stretch a balloon over the top. Line them up and launch a ping-pong ball, or marble, or whatever, through a tube, say a wrapping paper tube, and see how many pads can it bounce across.

Maddie: Some families did it with saucepans, we featured that in the show, and then that challenge caught on!

Greg: It's worth saying that making *Let's Go Live* meant so much to us as well. It helped get us through lockdown. And we built a community that we were getting to interact with every day. Stats wise, if you're wondering, I think shows were peaking at about 8,000 families watching live. So, that's maybe 15 or 20,000 people watching those shows live?!

Maddie: We had primary schools tuning in to cater for the children of key-workers. Some schools had 30 children of completely different year groups suddenly all being educated together, and *Let's Go Live* really helped. It meant that at 11am they could put the children in an assembly and the entire school could watch along with us. So it's actually really difficult for us to know our exact stats to be honest.

Greg: We say *Let's Go Live* got 3 million 'plays', and one play could be anything from one person

watching to a whole family, to a whole school. Our most popular episode was '*How to make a poo*', which was us in the spare room, using stuff you find around the house to recreate the full digestive system – and encouraging people to do the same! That's had over 200,000 plays. But for us, it was about the quality of the interaction and building that community rather than just an audience. We built this incredible community that actually then started supporting us making the shows.

Maddie: I would say for the first six weeks we were just putting our own money into making it happen.

Greg: There were costs involved… some bits of new tech etc, but also we had a graphics buddy who would do themed graphics each week, and we brought someone in to help edit the VTs.

Maddie: It hit a point where the show had become so big that it wasn't manageable for just the two of us without financial support anymore. So we started a crowd-funding Patreon, inviting our audience to support us with however much money they would like.

Greg: We wanted the show to be free, because we wanted anybody to be able to watch it and join us live or watch it back whenever.

Maddie: So thankfully, due to that community, we started getting a small pocket of money that came in from our Patrons. All of it went straight back into the show. We brought someone on board part-time to help manage the emails, because we simply didn't have time to write, produce, test, make VTs for a daily show, whilst also trying to look at 450 emails a day, and then turn that into user generated content.

Greg: But it was still only the two of us, in our house, writing the whole thing, making the props, testing everything, doing the tech. And of course hosting it. And also doing the back-end as well, the social and the thumbnails and all that jazz.

Maddie: There's a whole lot of metadata that goes into YouTube. We were constantly creating episode titles and thumbnails, rewriting titles for better with search engine optimisation (SEO). Originally our titles were episodic, but later we rewrote them to be searchable for teachers. And then we changed it again for a larger YouTube audience: What's the clicky YouTube title? All that upload and metadata stuff could be someone's full time job!

Greg: We've been asked "What did we lose from concentrating so much on *Let's Go Live*?" Well, we lost time, I guess, and we lost our minds, ha! When everyone else was doing their lockdown hobbies, or their Zoom quizzes, we were purely doing this and nothing else.

Maddie: We were riding the storm like everybody else, but we knew that there was a long-game and that we might eventually be able to step back, have a little bit more time for us; and at that point could consider, hey, does anybody want to work with us on this? But we didn't have time to approach anybody about sponsorship during lockdown; it wasn't until much later we had the bandwidth to do that.

Greg: It's worth a quick aside about the financials, because some people might be interested. YouTube is ad-based, and other people making content during lockdown were quite public about the considerable amount of money that they were getting from videos that were marketed at school children and families. We chose to market our content as 'made for kids', because it featured kids and was directed at kids. When you do that, you lose the ability to have personalised ads and your CPMs [cost per 1000 ad views] drop massively. So we had a video that had 20,000 views and we got like 5 quid.

Maddie: On a YouTube channel that has a very large library and a good number of views, I'd be quite happy to say, it pulls in about £300 a month…

Greg: …but because of this nature of 'made for kids', we shot ourselves in the foot by playing it by the book.

Maddie: However, when it comes to the community, I think about what we have gained.

It wasn't just for the duration of lockdown, it's a wonderful community who are still sticking with us now. Last summer we created a family science theatre show called *The Wonder Games*.

Greg: It was SO nice to meet the people that had supported us online; to actually meet them in real life.

Maddie: And because these were some of the most engaged families – they'd been sending in photos of that ridiculous game they had played or whatever activity they tried to make – we recognised them from the photos!

Greg: It was probably one of the most touching emotional experiences I've had through work. We did meet-and-greets after the theatre shows and they ended up being two hours the first day! But for us – to get to actually meet those *Let's Go Live* fans – that was so special.

When we got the sense that Lockdown 1 was going to lift soon, we kept pushing, didn't we? Was it 13 weeks, the first series? We kept going, and then we thought we'll keep going until schools start to go back. When lockdown lifted a bit, we paused for a short while, but then we thought we'd take the show out of the spare room!

Maddie: We switched our daily live shows for Saturday morning lives…

Greg: …which had always been an aspiration – to host and produce something like that. We did live shows from a farm, a forest, a computing museum, and our favourite, the walls of a mediaeval castle. These were one hour live shows, still fully interactive, full of quizzes, games and demos. Again just the two of us prepping all the tech, handling all the live stuff, doing all the vision mixing – it was amazing.

Those summer shows were incredible and we bumped into some *Let's Go Live*rs, who got wind of where we were gonna be, waving at us from the bottom of the castle.

Maddie: It was a fun challenge: we had to work out technically how to take everything that had been static in an office out and about without having a huge live team with us.

Greg: The first show, we ended up putting a mobile studio on a trailer on the back of a moving lawn mower. We started the show in the middle of a forest in our usual two-shot static approach, and then 10 minutes in, we went "Hang on!…" One of us disappeared and suddenly the studio was moving. We were on radio mics, so we could run off to a distant tree to measure it or whatever. I loved that tech challenge. And the number of messages we got from professionals saying, "How are you doing a multi-camera live vision mix, with graphics and sound cues, all from the walls of a castle whilst running around – just the two of you?!"

Maddie: And what's interesting for the makers of this software, is that we've really pushed the limits of it because the software is mostly used to live stream events and presentations for adults. But because we are using it to make kids' telly – and we want it to be as creative and educational as possible – we're using their functions in ways that they hadn't even considered.

Greg: To finish the timeline bit, fast forwarding, Lockdown 2 happened in January 2021.

Maddie: We had a dilemma, because we were being asked by the audience, "You're gonna help us, right? You're gonna come back and do more shows?" And we were like, "Are we?"

Greg: We weren't going to do it.

Maddie: We said "We can't do it to ourselves again!" Because we really did burn ourselves out last time. We were both sat on the sofa, and turned on the news to the announcement about Lockdown 2…

Greg: …and our phones went…

Maddie: …bzzz bzzz bzzz! And we looked at each other – "Ohhhhh, we've gotta do it."

Greg: We dropped to three days a week and did a whole new season, again with each week being themed.

Maddie: We had hoped that by doing three days a week, it would buy us more time for other projects, but of course it didn't. Rather than going to bed at 1am every day, we were going to bed at a normal time, but we were still working flat-out 5, if not 7, days a week.

Greg: By then we weren't as needed, as schools were back. So our live plays reduced to around 1,000, but lots of those were schools. Some were tuning in from all over the UK, and in Florida, California, Japan, and Australia!

Maddie: To finish the timeline, eventually Lockdown 2 ended and we all nervously went back out into the world. Our work ramped back up, and everybody was very, and rightfully so, bored of watching things online. *Let's Go Live* paused for a while. Since then we have been back with special episodes: we did specials for Halloween, Diwali and Christmas. We've also done some with sponsors: the Met Office approached us about making episodes on climate change and also the UKRI approached us about some vaccine related content. With

subjects like viruses, vaccines and climate change, we knew it would take a LOT of time and attention to get that scripting and messaging right for our audience. Having those sponsors onboard gave us experts that we could lean on, but also it gave us more time to really take care with such important topics.

Greg: In our vaccines content, we split the topic. The first episode was simply "*What are germs?*," because we had to start at the beginning. To understand a vaccine, you need to know what a germ is… what a virus is…

Maddie: And we did that in classic *Let's Go Live* style. We chose not to mention Covid at all. Instead, we created the 'Gregorious' virus and all of the learning was around this imaginary virus that was created between the two of us dressed up – me as a white blood cell and Greg as a virus.

Greg: And we were breaking into the house, which was the body. Going through the various stages of the nose. And getting covered in silly string – snot – and stuff like this.

Maddie: And because that was the basis of the learning, then we go, well, "*What is a vaccine then?*" It was all happening inside a friendly atmosphere. With the Met Office and talking about climate change, we were careful to not shy away from any of the facts, the realities, but to always approach everything in a way that was productive. We wanted to empower our audience. Some of the facts are really negative, but that doesn't mean we need to leave a child feeling like they can't do anything about it. So empowerment was the messaging that we ended up going for.

We made 84 themed episodes of *Let's Go Live*. Every single one of them had at least three hands-on science activities. Now we've taken each of those and put them on a free science activities website (www.letsgolivescience.com). Each activity has its own page, with a kit list, method, science, and links to the national curriculum. You can search them by topic. You can search them by theme. You can search them by age group or national curriculum link. That's something else we decided to make off the back of *Let's Go Live*, because we think it's helpful for teachers, home-schoolers – anyone looking for something to entertain the kids!

People still say to us, "Why did nobody pick this up? Like why have the BBC not picked this up?" And the reality is the BBC were very busy creating *Bitesize*. But because they are a huge organisation, it took the whole of Lockdown 1 to do that. We were fortunate to be able to go from day one. We couldn't have done that if it wasn't just us two.

Greg: We'd had two seasons of shows out when *Bitesize* went live I think, and *Bitesize* still had the feel of a traditional broadcast set up. Whereas part of the appeal of *Let's Go Live* was that these two familiar, trusted, faces would always be there doing fun things in their spare room.

Maddie: *Let's Go Live* was something very special that came out of that time, for that time.

How to Make a Poo!

How to make Fireworks in a Jar

How to make a Solar Oven for S'mores

Pirate Dave Ghost Scope

is proud to support the Children's Media Foundation and **doubly** chuffed to be part of CMC 2022 in Sheffield!

The World According To GRANDPA

Double award-winning!

WINNER
Best Pre-School Programme

VLV Voice of the Listener & Viewer

Best Children's Programme 2022 Winner

The Wonton Warrior

Proud to be a double _international_ Nominee for our CBBC drama The Wonton Warrior

Come and see us at saffroncherryproductions.co.uk - Visit Us

Cecilia Persson Takes the Children's Media Yearbook inside the **New BBC Studios Kids & Family Division**

Cecilia Persson, Managing Director, Kids & Family, BBC Studios Productions

I've always hugely admired the BBC. Growing up in Sweden, I fondly remember watching the *Magic Roundabout* and *Paddington Bear*. So having the chance to work here, to be involved in creating even more exciting and beloved content for children – and to be instrumental in introducing these wonderful shows to other kids all around the world – feels like an amazing opportunity, and a privilege. Especially with the move of BBC Children's In-House Productions into BBC Studios to form the new Kids & Family division, which enables us to be even more ambitious in growing the value we provide to younger audiences. Here I feel my passion for kids' content and brands, coupled with my commercial broadcast experience in the sector, gives me the ideal background to drive BBC Studios Kids & Family forward. I'm responsible for our overall strategy – shaping and implementing strategy is one of my strengths – along with our creative health, pipeline and production capability, reporting into Ralph Lee, CEO of BBC Studios Production who oversees our four production genres: Scripted, Formats, Factual and Kids & Family. In this new role, I want to forge deeper relationships with our biggest customer, BBC Children's; seek out fresh ideas and create exciting new partnerships with top talent; and deliver value in terms of reputation and income back to the BBC.

The transfer of BBC Children's In-House productions into BBC Studios Productions is an exciting development that sees BBC Studios Kids & Family uniquely positioned to become a major global force in children's content. It marries our brilliant content creators and production capabilities with outstanding commercial expertise, creating an even more exciting content offering for our commissioners and buyers and enhancing our offer to on- and off-screen creative talent, who'll be able to work with us in a variety of ways. Importantly, it also generates excellent development opportunities for our team and for our freelance colleagues. It means we're now in the best position to invest competitively in the content and creators we need to grow. Bold British creativity is at the heart of BBC Studios and it's crucial to nurture the next generation of talent.

Pulling all of BBC Studios together, we can now see content through its full life cycle, from development, commissioning, production and co-production through to sales, consumer products, digital and distribution, maximising the potential of BBC-owned IP. This expertise will increase the reach of in-house hits and grow and develop new global brands. I'm confident that our 'One Portfolio' approach to content across all four genres in BBC Studios Productions will drive and empower great success.

We already have a truly exceptional, incredibly diverse portfolio of children's content that is globally renowned and beloved by kids and their families. Now we want to build on that to create the *Blue Peters*, *Tracy Beakers* and *Hey Duggees* of the future, that will resonate equally deeply with children across the UK and beyond. We never forget that the stories we tell have the power to make a difference to our audience; it's what makes us so passionate about our content and drives us to deliver the highest quality we can. We're constantly striving to produce fresh, rich and imaginative content that connects with British children and families, and that also has the potential to be a worldwide hit. There's so much brilliant creativity and expertise within the division to spearhead innovation and growth. We are also privileged to be able to work with some of the biggest, best and most-loved talent around, and it's really exciting to discover new and diverse voices who could become the stars of tomorrow.

BBC Children's will remain Kids & Family's biggest focus and we will continue to collaborate closely with Patricia Hidalgo, Director of BBC Children's and Education, and her team to provide them with a wealth of content and shows that will connect with and thrill their audience the length and breadth of the UK, and stay with them as they grow up.

And BBC Studios Kids & Family is also open for business across the whole industry, creating an end-to-end business of scale and reputation with the potential to work for a wide range of customers. We have a mixed focus, spread across production, distribution and consumer. On the production side, we're really keen to explore new co-production opportunities – for example, potentially partnering on high-cost projects – and we're always on the look-out for fresh ideas and new talent. With exceptional expertise in distribution and franchise management, we're looking to expand these activities too.

It's a really exciting time for us and these changes will provide unique opportunities for our customers and our talent. They will allow us to extend the footprint of Kids & Family, forging additional partnerships with other platforms and broadcasters.

They will help us achieve our ambition – to create the very best content for children and their families – and to be a vital part of young people's lives. We want to continue the remarkable BBC legacy of producing top-quality content that delivers the hits of today and the nostalgia of the future, and we want to align execution across the business to maximise this content. By cultivating commercial and creative growth, we build value for younger BBC audiences. Our content is bold, vibrant and engaging – and our future as BBC Kids & Family will be too.

Image: BBC Studios Production

The Seven Secrets of a Successful Pitch

Paul Boross, The Pitch Doctor and Humourologist

The art of the pitch is a valuable set of skills that can serve you in any walk of life. Whether you are in business or entertainment, building the ability to pitch your ideas will directly result in more success. These tips and tricks will help you win over your audience and convince others that your clever ideas are the key. Here are the seven secrets to any successful pitch and how to hone them to meet your goals.

1. Enjoy being nervous

Making a pitch can be a nerve-racking experience. Nervousness is a completely natural response to presenting your important ideas in front of an audience. Although it may not feel like it, nervousness is a valuable feeling. It means that you're connected with what's really going on and can evaluate the importance of the situation. Once you identify that nervousness is a good thing because it means that you're doing something that matters, you can begin enjoying the feeling. It even starts to feel like excitement! If you aren't nervous it means that you think that what you are doing isn't worth it. Embrace your nervous feelings and use them to make your pitch more powerful.

2. Understand why you are there

The biggest mistake of any pitch is when the speaker tries to convince the audience that they are there for a good reason. You do not have to convince the audience that they should listen to you. They are already in the room and ready to hear what you have to say. They have already made their decision, you don't have to convince them again. Understand that you are there to pitch your ideas and ensure that your audience understands what you have to say. When you understand why you are there, you will better utilise your time to present your ideas in a complete and captivating way. Your ideas are great, let them speak for themselves. When you understand your reason for being in the room, it becomes easier to open up your pitch into a conversation. When you include your audience in your pitch, they will quickly see that you are the expert. Your personability will make your pitch shine in a positive light.

3. Get to know your audience

The internet makes it easy to do your research before you give a pitch. Be sure to take the time out to learn everything you can about the people you are pitching to. You may be able to include some personalised information that helps sell your pitch. If you are pitching to a company, it is important to know that company's values before you craft your pitch. Although you shouldn't change your ideas based on your audience, understanding them is a key component to crafting a creative, compelling, and complete pitch which is music to their ears.

You can even get to know your audience while you are pitching. Include a few questions and jokes and watch how the audience responds. As you learn to listen and build the ability to read the room, you will be able to deliver a perfect pitch every time.

4. Plan to use less time than allotted

No matter how many times you practise, your pitch will never last exactly as long as you think. The goal of a pitch is to present all of the information you have within the given time. You cannot do this if your pitch goes long or you get cut off for going over time. Add to this the fact that, when you're talking, you're not watching the time and you'll be using far more in the real pitch than you did when you practised. This is why you should plan your pitch to be shorter than the time you are provided. Your audience will be grateful that you were able to convey your ideas succinctly, saving them time in their busy schedules.

This also allows for more conversation around your ideas after your pitch. These conversations may be the key to making a connection that will influence your pitch's success.

5. Create connections

Audiences will be more willing to buy in to your message if they feel you are relatable or likeable. Try to create connections with your audience during your pitch. One of the easiest ways to do this is to make your audience laugh.

Photo: by Kenny Eliason on Unsplash

Genuine laughter brings people together and if you don't feel that you can tell a joke, at least approach your pitch in a light hearted way so that they will be more likely to pay close attention to the rest of your presentation. Adding a question and answer section within your pitch is a great way to spark conversations where connection can be created. You can then incorporate the information gathered in the Q&A section to give a killer conclusion that will sell your audience on your pitch.

6. Ask for what you want

A pitch is a place to persuade your audience to give you what you want. Too often, presenters will beat around the bush without saying what it is they are there to accomplish. Make sure that your pitch states clearly what it is you want. Do not leave it to your audience to connect the dots. Be clear and concise and simply ask for the things you want and which you feel are also in the best interests of your audience. Once your audience is clear on what you are looking for they will be much more willing to give it to you. Ask for what you want clearly and concisely at least once in your pitch, preferably at the start of your pitch so that your audience can then figure out how to help you get it, and how it helps them too.

7. Follow up and follow through

The pitch is often your first impression, but it by no means needs to be your last. Take the time to follow up after the pitch. Thank your audience for sharing your time and see if they have any questions for you now that they have had time to sit with your pitch for a while. A follow up conversation can help remind your audience who you are and what you are all

about. Following up shows that your pitch is meaningful to you and a great follow up may be the difference between winning the pitch and being forgotten. At the very least, you're showing that you're committed and that it's important to you.

In addition to following up after a pitch, be sure to follow through on the actions you've promised. Whether that means continuing to develop your idea or contacting additional parties, following through on your promises shows everyone that you are committed to transforming your pitch into actions, and most importantly, that you are the kind of person who does what you say you will do.

Deliver a powerful and positive pitch with practice

These seven secrets of a successful pitch will only bring your powerfully positive results if you practise. Find a partner or a friend and practise your pitch as much as you can. Keep these secrets in mind by building yourself a practice checklist and you will be sure to deliver a pitch that people love every time.

Although these secrets will bring your pitch to the next level, nothing beats being prepared, personable and positive. When you lead with a sense of humour and an openness of personality you will win over any audience you stand in front of. Begin with conversation and let your preparation speak for itself. If you present yourself as likeable, your audience will be more willing to be on your side. Present a powerful pitch by putting people first.

Adaptation

Jayne Kirkham, Writer and Script Consultant

It's probably fair to say that most intellectual properties for children these days are developed with several media in mind. 'Three-sixty' was a buzz word for a while, until it sounded too 'buzzy' and, anyway, 'multi-platform' content was now taken as a given. But what if you're a novelist by trade or remember a book from your own childhood that you want to bring to a new audience?

Adaptation. It's an art you know. There are textbooks that say so. Books like *The Art of Adaptation* by Linda Seger (1992). There are theories, like *A Theory of Adaptation* by Linda Hutcheon (2012); crumbs, there's even an Oxford Handbook! Although to be fair that's a *Handbook of Adaptation Studies* (Leitch, ed, 2020). People study adaptation!

What are we talking about here? I'll define adaptation as taking an intellectual property from one medium and using it in another. And Linda Seger is right. It is an art.

It is easy to forget that there are fundamental differences in the ways different media communicate their ideas to an audience. At the risk of teaching you to suck eggs:

- Literary works use words to spark the reader's imagination to create atmospheres, images, sounds, even scents, using the past, present and yes even the future tense. Because it all happens in the reader's mind, the world of the story can be anywhere and be presented in varying degrees of detail, depending on the literary aspirations and needs of the book (or magazine or newspaper article). The author can take the reader inside the heads of the people they're writing about so we know their thoughts.

- Theatrical works use light, sound, set and performers to convey meaning. Bound by time and space (the length of the play, the size of the auditorium), the world of the story can be simple thumbnail suggestions or replicate an actual place. Nevertheless, it is a time and space shared with the audience. The character, through the performer, can tell the spectator what they are thinking and what they want.

- Whereas theatre can only give a sense of the story world, the screen gives the illusion of reality, wherever and whatever that reality may be. Screenworks were once absolutely time bound; dependent in the black and white days on the length of a movie reel, or broadcasting slots. Now with viewing on demand, traditional broadcast slots are arguably a thing of the past. But think of Tiktok or all those boxsets that get binge-watched. You need to tell your story quick before that thumb scrolls to the next. And even the bingiest of binge-watchers needs a break to go to the loo. But what remains the same is the fact that screen-based stories are completely dependent on what is shown on screen, the images, to create meaning.

- While direct address is sometimes used in screen-based fiction, for the most part, the audience only knows what a character is thinking because of what they see them doing. Small screens and the more industrial nature of TV production mean that there is more talk than in films but even so, what is important is what we see. And what we see is in the present tense. Yes, there may be flashbacks, but even flashbacks are told in the present tense.

This difference is why many brilliant novels, journals, magazine articles simply don't transfer well to the screen: too much – the desires, the conflicts, the ideas – is going on inside the character and the camera can't see it. In order for a literary text to work on screen, all those conflicts, desires and ideas need externalising.

Of course, now we have a further medium to consider adapting: the computer game. This is already a form of screen-based storytelling but the fundamental difference here is that the viewer plays an active part in the unfolding of the narrative. Simply switching the characters to a passive medium like a film or TV series is not that simple. Remember the *Moshi Monsters*? A Massively Multiplayer Online Role Playing Game with over 80 million registered users back in the day. I was invited to submit episode ideas for a TV series they were developing. This was about the same time that they released a feature film, it was all very exciting. But try as we might, giving good stories to the characters was like nailing jelly to a wall. If I remember correctly, it came down to the rules of the story world: while they worked with an active participant in the game, in a passive TV narrative, they left too many holes for the characters' credibility to

fall through. The world seemed to work better in the film but it didn't do well. Mark Kermode said it was "Baffling, disturbing and boring for the over-fives."

Having recognised this difference between the media, the question then is, where do you start? Probably with whatever it is that you want to adapt. And probably with the question, why do you want to adapt it? To bring it to a wider audience? To make a large wodge of dosh? Because you think it would be better told in a different way? All three?

> Only you can answer that and it is important that you do, because you're likely to be working on this project for a long time.

The answer to the next question could stop the whole project in its tracks: do you have permission to adapt the source material? Who holds the copyright? It is vital to find out and track them down before going any further. It may take some detective work but the first place to look will be the copyright statement (usually at the front or rear of a publication) or look on the publisher's website. Check databases from the Society of Authors UK and WATCH (Writers, Artists, and their Copyright Holders). Once you know who the copyright owner is, you will need to contact them to request permission. Without their permission you can do nothing.

Let's assume you have permission.

Having committed to a project, what is needed next is a thorough understanding of the source material. What makes it work in the form it is in? Who are the characters? What are their individual stories? What theme arises out of those stories to control the whole narrative? What genre is it? How is the story structured? What is its narrative style? What is original about it? Which of those things do you want to transfer to your screen version? That depends on how faithful you want to be to the original. And you don't have to be: Disney's *The Jungle Book* (1967) comes to mind. Are there things that you simply can't afford to lose?

Next comes thinking about the medium you are going to use. If it's a movie, is there too much story to fit into 90 minutes or thereabouts? If it's a serial for TV/online, is there enough for a given number of episodes? If it is for a returnable series, will the characters generate enough extra stories for all those episodes down the line? You may need to create new characters in keeping with the original cast. You may need to kill some off. Given that the story telling needs to be visual, you may need to create a whole load of new scenes. Many years ago, I was commissioned to turn Ann Kelley's 2007 Costa Children's Book Award-winning novel, *The Bowerbird*, into a screenplay. It's the haunting story of a child waiting for a heart and lung transplant: living on death's edge while trying to be an ordinary kid. While the story is a roller-coaster of emotion for the reader, there is not a lot of physical action for a film. I was fortunate in that I had the pre- and se-quels to draw on and Ann's permission to reshape the story to entertain a family audience while not losing the heart (excuse the pun) of the original text. But that meant quite a lot of invention.

The film was never made. Why? The feedback I remember, when the producer was looking for financiers, was that it was too dark for a young audience. Gussie the main character was 12 and while children that age might read about her in a book, in a film they want something more… fun. Staying true to the books is all very well, but perhaps you need to stay truer to your audience.

All of us working in children's media know the importance of this. But it is easy to forget, especially when working with material from our own childhood or what might be termed 'heritage works'. But the children growing up now have a completely

Photo: Radarsmum67 on Flickr

Photo: by Rod Long on Unsplash

different perspective on life to us grown-ups. They have never known a world without the internet or where corporal punishment was a regular occurrence in schools. They have never known a world where bullying or casual racism or sexism were unquestioned and even considered funny.

I recently adapted *A Little Princess* by Frances Hodgson Burnett for audio. First published in 1905, it is set against the backdrop of the British Raj, with the heroine Sara Crewe coming from India to go to a boarding school in England. It is a world of cruel race and class differentiation that children today would not recognise and was hardly appropriate for a bedtime story. That doesn't mean I modernised the setting. Far from it. This was still Edwardian England, but with anything anachronistic to a modern child shaded out. So, there was still a dramatic story of a rich little girl who, despite losing everything and living as little more than a slave, remains kind and loving, standing up for those even worse off than herself, and is justly rewarded at the end, without the cruel beatings and violent language.

Adapting your favourite novel or comic book hero, for the screen; spending time with, albeit imaginary, people you love should be a joy. But what really matters is the final product: will your audience find spending time with those characters as much of a joy? There will no doubt be diehard fans of the source material who will spit on your grave for daring to touch their beloved. But, and this is especially true for the young audience, there will be many that are meeting those characters for the first time. And if you have done a decent job, they will be falling in love with them too.

References

Seger, L. (1992) *The Art of Adaptation.* Holt Paperbacks

Hutcheon, L. (2012) *A Theory of Adaptation.* Routledge

Leitch, T. (ed) (2020) *The Oxford Handbook of Adaptation Studies.* Oxford University Press

Acton-Smith, M. (2016) I was Mr Stress, Now I'm Mr Calm. *The Telegraph*, April 2.

Kermode, M. (2013) Moshi Monsters: the Movie - review. *The Guardian,* December 22.

Rick Jones

Frederick James (Rick) Jones, 1937–2021

Canadian born Frederick (Rick) Jones was known to a generation of children as a co-presenter of *Play School* but came into his own as the smooth-toned storyteller 'Yoffy' on *Fingerbobs*.

Rick trained at the Webber Douglas School of Singing and Dramatic Art from the age of 18 and after appearing in *Spoon River* at the Royal Court Theatre in 1964, in which he sang and played guitar, he was invited to present *Play School* by the creator Joy Whitby who was in the audience.

Rick presented 447 episodes of *Play School* from 1964–1973 but it was as the puppeteer and storyteller 'Yoffy' that he is remembered most fondly. Although only 13 episodes were made it was repeated often until 1984.

After *Fingerbobs* Rick joined the British country rock band Meal Ticket and co-wrote many of their songs. They were popular on the London pub circuit and released three albums. Rick also co-wrote the theme songs for *The Aeronauts* and 'You'd Better Believe It, Babe' for *The Flipside of Dominick Hide,* as well as co-writing two musicals, *Captain Crash vs the Zzorg Women Chapters 5 & 6*, which enjoyed a six-week run in Los Angeles in 1981, and *Laughing Daughter*, based on the songs of Meal Ticket.

Rick was gifted in so many ways. Not only as an actor and singer, but as a songwriter, a musician, a storyteller, an author, an artist, a sculptor, a cartoonist, and a loving father, brother, husband and grandfather. He was interested in people and was an interesting man, generous with his time and full of worldly wisdom.

He released 13 music albums in total, the last of which was completed the day before he died. He gave it the thumbs up and passed away in his wife Valerie's arms, with his two daughters close by. A life well lived. Rest in peace my friend.

Remembered by **Garry Vaux**, Cartoonist, Artist and Illustrator

Theresa Plummer-Andrews

Theresa Plummer-Andrews (known as Trees or Plum), who sadly died aged 77 on 31st August 2021, was one of the greats of the children's animation world.

She was a relative late-comer to children's TV. I first met her in 1981 in the London offices of TVS International (Television South was then the ITV franchise holder for the South and South East of England). I was heading TVS's embryonic Children's department. Trees had previously worked in a theatrical agency, whose clients included Richard Burton and Elizabeth Taylor, and on the live action TV series *Elephant Boy*, but had no particular interest in kids' programming. However I asked her to look at a few scripts we were assessing, and she became intrigued.

From then on she quickly became more involved in animation, and when I returned to the BBC in 1986 I asked her to join our acquisitions team. She steadily built up the team, and in partnership with BBC Worldwide managed to considerably increase our investment in original animation.

As both Producer and Executive Producer her numerous credits reflect some of the best and most loved animation of the time: *Noddy*, *Fireman Sam*, *Bob the Builder*, *Postman Pat*, *Pingu* etc. She was particularly proud of *The Animals of Farthing Wood*, a big and complicated pan-European co-production.

Theresa Plummer-Andrews, 1944–2021

After retiring from the BBC, Trees set up a consultancy and remained involved with the industry, also spending time visiting and partying with her numerous friends all over the world.

Trees was often outspoken, tenacious about her projects, fiercely loyal to her friends and colleagues, generous, much respected and enormous fun. The world will be much quieter without her.

There have been many tributes to her from colleagues and friends. Nigel Pickard writes "such sad news that one of the true legends of the kids' business is no longer with us. She was wonderfully outspoken, but her undoubted passion, creativity and humour were her defining qualities, and she had a brilliant grasp of what would work for the audience. Theresa, we will hugely miss you." We all echo that thought.

Remembered by **Anna Home OBE**, Chair, The Children's Media Foundation

David McKee

David McKee, 1935–2022

When David McKee died in April this year, much was written about his work as an author and illustrator. And rightly so – he worked prodigiously and created more than 50 picture books including *Not Now Bernard* and of course, the mighty *Elmer*. David was still working when he died and imagining him without a pen or a brush in his hand is, simply, unimaginable.

However, few of those obituaries mentioned the enormous contribution he made to children's television. Alongside his decades-long working relationship and friendship with his publisher Klaus Flugge at Anderson Press was his parallel career with producer Clive Juster. Clive and David met in the late 1960s when they worked on the legendary series *Mr Benn* and from those early days working from David's flat in Barnes they continued to collaborate, firstly on a series of short films for Save the Children, and then on the series produced through the company they set up in 1979 with animator Leo Nielsen, King Rollo Films. That body of work is remarkable in itself – *King Rollo, Victor & Maria, Towser, The Adventures of Spot, Watt the Devil, Ric the Raven, Maisy*. David designed and

wrote and even performed vocals for some of them, but they did more than simply make the films. Renting the smallest stand in the Palais, off they went to Cannes to MIP TV to stand shoulder-to-shoulder with the big distributors and sell them, too. Whilst Clive took meetings, David would be found with a glass of wine in one hand and a paintbrush in the other, decorating the stand with paintings of that year's project. King Rollo Films was the first British Indie specialising in children's media, regularly selling to over 100 countries and gaining an international reputation of excellence. Working for King Rollo Films at the start of my career, I loved Dave's naughtiness, his delight in discovery, his gentleness and stubbornness, and his love of winding up journos who printed interviews without questioning whether he really was the son of brandy smugglers or tap-dancing pirates. David famously spurned technology, rejecting email and the internet and living always in the present. He communicated with the same joy and delight that he brought to his books and films and I was the lucky recipient of some of his famously decorated envelopes with the address and stamp worked into the design. I have no idea how the postman ever delivered them.

David often said in interviews that he was selfish, that he did everything for himself. In a way that was true, as he built a life for himself based on never having to do what his mother would have called a 'proper job'. And he certainly never did anything to please anyone else. But for anyone who has ever opened one of his books or watched one of his films it is immediately apparent that his generosity of spirit, his love of storytelling, his ability to use humour and colour to make people think about important issues such as racism, accepting difference or the futility of war, was anything but selfish. David taught me that children deserve the best, to never underestimate their ability to decipher meaning and not to fear ambiguity so that the work continues to live and breathe and merit re-reading or watching. His legacy is a body of enduring stories and characters that children will carry with them through their lives. A gift indeed.

Remembered by **Lucy Murphy**, Director of Kids Content, Sky

Contributors

Japhat Asher

Japhet Asher is the director of Polarity Reversal Ltd, a content creation and consulting company that is currently developing new tech to link physical books and digital tools.

He is an Executive Producer, creative leader and collaborative storyteller with over 30 years experience as an innovator of formats, products, and narrative experiences across genres and platforms. He is an Oscar nominated documentary maker, a creator of Emmy winning animation, developed and led digital platforms for BBC Children's, and is author of the world's first AR powered novel. He is a passionate advocate for content that challenges, informs, and entertains, connecting memorable characters and experiences to their audiences, most notably children and young adults.

Margaret Bartley

Margaret Bartley is Editorial Director at Bloomsbury Publishing for Classics, Drama & Performance and Literary Studies. She has worked in academic publishing for over 30 years as a commissioning editor in Literary Studies, Linguistics, History and Study Skills. Since 2002 she has been the Publisher of the Arden Shakespeare and now has editorial responsibility for Bloomsbury's digital platform Drama Online, the Methuen Drama imprint, and the Arden Shakespeare. She

is Bloomsbury's representative on the Lit in Colour Advisory Board and sponsor of Bloomsbury Academic's Diversity, Equity and Inclusion working group.

Katie Battersby

Katie Battersby joined the research team KidsKnowBest in September 2021 as a Research Executive, supporting the execution of project work on behalf of brands looking to gain insight about their young consumers and audiences.

Paul Boross

Paul Boross is an inspirational business psychologist and Humourologist who packs a punchline.

Paul – aka The Pitch Doctor – has refined the art of making corporate audiences laugh while they learn, communicating the most vital messages at an emotional level that stays with people, long after the event comes to a close.

Drawing on a career that has taken him from primetime TV, music and stand-up comedy to business, consultancy and motivational psychology, he trains companies, celebrities and executives in the art and craft of communication.

Paul's frontline experience of performance at London's legendary Comedy Store and strong commercial instincts enable him to deliver focused and effective training to clients from across the industry spectrum, from

the BBC to Barclays via Google, Nestlé, WPP, Virgin and MTV.

Paul is a much in demand international keynote speaker and trainer. His four bestselling books on pitching and communication continue to sit high in the Amazon charts. Early next year, his fifth book, *Humourology – The Serious Business of Comedy at Work*, will be released with contributions by some of the world's most renowned business leaders and comedians.

For more tips on how to put the fun back into business fundamentals, check out *The Humourology Podcast* (Humourology.com) available wherever you get your podcasts. The glittering line up fantastic guests provide a plethora of pitching and business knowledge that you can't find anywhere else.

www.PaulBoross.com

Dr Cynthia Carter

Cynthia Carter is Reader in the School of Journalism, Media and Culture, Cardiff University, UK. She has published widely on children, news and citizenship; young people and public service broadcasting; and feminist news and journalism studies. Her most recent book is *Journalism, Gender and Power* (Routledge, 2019). She is a founding Co-Editor of Feminist Media Studies and serves on the editorial board of numerous media and communication studies journals.

Jo Claessens

Jo is the Series Producer on *BBC Tiny Happy People*, a key provision in the BBC's levelling up framework – developing strong foundations in the early years. She leads a multidisciplinary team responsible for all commissioned content, campaign, web & social output and outreach activity across the service. Jo has produced many high profile campaigns for BBC Education including *BBC Terrific Scientific* and *BBC micro:bit*. Before joining the BBC, Jo was a publisher for Granada, ITV after making a switch from teaching in 2000, having trained and taught as a primary school teacher specialising in Early Years for almost 10 years.

Dr Máire Messenger Davies

Máire Messenger Davies is Emerita Professor of Media Studies and Policy at Ulster University. She has a BA in English from Trinity College Dublin and, after a journalistic career in local newspapers and national magazines, she obtained a PhD in psychology at the University of East London, studying how audiences learn from television. She has worked at Boston University and at the University of Pennsylvania in the USA and, later, in the School of Journalism, Media and Cultural Studies at Cardiff University. She specialises in the study of child media audiences and is the author of several books including *Children, Media and Culture* (McGraw Hill/Open University, 2010); *"Dear BBC": Children, Television Storytelling and the Public Sphere* (Cambridge University Press, 2001); *Television is Good for Your Kids* (Hilary Shipman, (1989, 2002); and, with Roberta Pearson, *Star Trek and American Television* (University of California Press, 2014). She has four grown-up children and three grandchildren. She lives with her journalist husband in Cardiff, Wales. She is a Patron of the Children's Media Foundation.

Sebastian Debertin

Sebastian Debertin is acting as KiKA's Head of International Content, Acquisitions & Co-Productions, responsible for all international fiction, non-fiction and pre-school content.

Sebastian, who helped launch KiKA more than 25 years ago, is an Emmy award-winning, highly experienced creative producer of a broad variety of children's media. He has produced, co-produced, commissioned or acquired world-class live action programs like many times award-winning series *KRIMI.DE* and *Annedroids* as well as highly successful animated programs like *Guess How Much I Love You?*, *Chloé's Closet*, *Yakari*, *Blinky Bill*, *Tib & Tumtum*, *Insectibles* just to name a few, and reaching outstanding ratings success with kids between 3–13+ years for KiKA. He is currently the Executive Producer for animated shows like *The Smurfs* with Dupuis, IMPS-Peyo Productions, Ketnet & TF1, *Dog Loves Books* with iGeneration Studios (aka Komixx Entertainment) and the BBC, *Odo* with Letko Prod., Poland, Sixteen South from Northern Ireland and Milkshake, as well as pre-school series *Mumfie* with Zodiak Kids, Animoka Studios, Italy, and Italian public broadcaster RAI. New co-pros in 2023 include *Goat Girl* with Daily Madness Productions from Ireland and Miam !, France, with Discovery-Warner Media. Sebastian also enjoys sharing his broad expertise with the next generation of media producers at various Schools and Universities.

Greg Foot

Greg Foot is an award-winning Science Journalist, Producer & Presenter, writing, hosting & producing science content on TV, radio, YouTube, podcast, and stage for 15+ years: from investigative documentaries on TV, Radio & Podcasts; to ambitious interactive live shows for families on YouTube; to eye-catching experiments on live TV; and engaging keynotes & spectacular science shows on stages around the world.

A scientist by training (first class degree in Natural Sciences from Cambridge University), Greg is also Creative Director of digital-first production studio sciencemedia.studio and a Wellcome Trust Public Engagement Fellow.

Joe Godwin

Joe joined BBC Children's as a trainee in 1989, becoming an assistant producer, studio director and producer on shows such as *Record Breakers*, *Going Live* and *Blue Peter*. In 1997 he became Editor of Children's Presentation before joining Nickelodeon in 2000, where he had a number of jobs including Head of Original Production and Interactive Director.

Joe returned to the BBC in 2005 as Head of Children's Entertainment, then Head of News, Factual and Entertainment. In 2009 he was appointed as Director, BBC Children's, responsible for all of the BBC's services for children. He led the department's move from London to Salford in 2011.

In 2015 Joe left the world of children's media after 25 years to become Director, BBC Midlands and the BBC Academy. In 2020 he took up the role of Director of Partnerships for BBC Nations & Regions, responsible for key partnerships across the UK – including the Commonwealth Games and UK City of Culture.

In 2021, despite being far too young, he retired and got a whippet called Dylan.

Gavin Halpin

Gavin Halpin is the Managing Director of Paper Owl Films, which he co-founded in 2012. Since graduating with a first class honours degree in Film and Communications from the Dublin Institute of Technology, Gavin has produced hundreds of television programmes and his experience has given him a unique perspective on the creativity, resilience, and belief it takes to create award winning content.

Gavin is a driving force in Paper Owl Films as the key business affairs contact and Executive Producer. Along with being an active member of the board of Screen Producers Ireland, Gavin sits on the Children's TV Council for Screen Skills UK.

Rebekkah Hughes

Rebekkah is Design Manager for Oriel Square, a strategy, research and publishing specialist focused on education. Rebekkah oversees the creative side of Oriel Square's design projects, including resource management, commissioning artwork, illustrators and designers, as well as fulfilling internal design needs. This is the first time she has designed the *Children's Media Yearbook*.

Jayne Kirkham

With over 20 years' experience screenwriting and 14 years teaching at the Northern Film School and other universities, Jayne has written both original work and adaptations for features, TV, and audio. Commissions include Marina Lewycka's *Two Caravans* for Blue Zoo, Anne Kelley's *The Bowerbird* for Artemisia Films. Most recently she has retold classic novels and tales such as *Black Beauty* and *Pinocchio* for Toniebox, and is currently a member of HoHo Entertainment's writing team for a forthcoming animated series. Jayne is a member of The Children's Media Foundation Board and on their behalf volunteers as Clerk to the All-Party Parliamentary Group for Children's Media and the Arts.

Hannie Kirkham

Hannie Kirkham is Research and Business Development Manager for Oriel Square, a strategy, research and publishing specialist focused on education. Hannie leads the Research team, driving market research and product development alongside thought leadership publications and events. She has over ten years experience in educational publishing for print and digital media in the UK and internationally, and is a primary school governor. Hannie also has an interest in the intersection between children's education and entertainment and has worked with the Children's Media Conference as Newsletter Editor, Blogger and Producer. This is her first Co-Editorship for the *Children's Media Yearbook*.

David Kleeman

Strategist, analyst, author, speaker, connector – David Kleeman has led the children's media industry in developing sustainable, child-friendly practices for 35 years. He began this work as president of the American Centre for Children and Media and is now Senior Vice President of Global Trends for Dubit, a strategy/research consultancy and digital studio.

When he began this work, 'children's media' meant television. Today, he is fascinated by, and passionate about, kids' wide range of possibilities for entertainment, engagement, play and learning. David uses research, insights and experience to show that much may change, but children's developmental path and needs remain constant. David is advisory board chair to the international children's TV festival PRIX JEUNESSE, on the board of the Children's Media Association (USA) and the Advisory Board of the Joan Ganz Cooney Centre. He has served as a Senior Fellow of the Fred Rogers Centre and Board Vice President for the National Association for Media Literacy Education.

Prof Sonia Livingstone

Prof Sonia Livingstone DPhil (Oxon), FBA, FBPS, FAcSS, FRSA, OBE is a professor in the Department of Media and Communications at the London School of Economics and Political Science.

She is the author of 20 books on children's online opportunities and risks, including *The Class: Living and Learning in the Digital Age*. Sonia has advised the UK government, European Commission, European Parliament, Council of Europe and other national and international organisations on children's rights, risks and safety in the digital age.

Genevieve Margrett

Genevieve Margrett is albert's Communications Manager. She inadvertently joined the project back in 2011 when she was part of BAFTAs communication team and was asked to help 'quickly' bring the project to life but stayed working with the small team in

those first few years as she could see how much potential the project had to grow.

Following stints with Harvey Nichols and Diageo, Genevieve re-joined the albert team in 2018 and has enjoyed working to grow albert's presence in the industry. More recently she helped to bring a series of events to COP26, including the pan-broadcaster Climate Content Pledge announcement.

Dr Jane Mavoa

Dr Jane Mavoa is an academic researcher in Australia interested in children's digital game play, datafication, online privacy and digital inclusion.

Gráinne McGuinness

Gráinne McGuinness is an award winning creator of standout stories for young children that encourage them to see the world in different ways. As Creative Director at Paper Owl Films, Gráinne leads the development of ambitious content for international audiences.

Creator of *Pablo* for CBeebies and RTÉJr., the series is celebrated all over the world for its timely portrayal of a smart little autistic character. She is currently developing Series 3, with a colourful musical theatre show in the works and a series of ladybird books with Penguin Random House.

Current projects include *Sol*, a special about a young boy on a quest to bring the light back to the world after the death of his beloved grandmother and

Ladybird & Bee, a first-hand view of nature from two little friends in Wild Meadow. She is creator of brand new *Happy the Hoglet* due on CITV October 2022. Credits also include two series of preschool cookery show *Bia Linn* for TG4 & 8–12s cookery with *Ár mBia Ár Slí* for RTÉJr.

Maddie Moate

Maddie Moate is a BAFTA-winning presenter and YouTuber, passionate about curiosity. She is the host of the BAFTA-nominated CBeebies TV series *Maddie's Do You Know?*, BBC Earth's *Earth Unplugged*, CBBC's *Show Me the Honey* and Fully Charged's YouTube series *Maddie Goes Electric*.

Maddie is one of the few family-focused "Edu-tubers" in the UK and has been creating fun, educational, science videos for the past 8 years. She has amassed over 190 thousand subscribers and 50+ million views on her YouTube channel which is also the home of *Let's Go Live with Maddie and Greg*, a popular live science show for families and children of all ages.

In 2020 Maddie launched her podcast *Maddie's Sound Explorers* with Sony Music. Each episode explores the sounds of science and nature as Maddie is joined by experts who guide the listeners on all kinds of journeys.

Maddie is also a published non-fiction children's author and writes and performs her own theatre shows. Over the years she has enjoyed acting in the CBeebies Christmas shows, Ballets, and the CBeebies Prom at the Royal Albert Hall.

Lucy Murphy

Lucy Murphy is the Director of Kids Content at Sky. Lucy's role includes acquisitions and original content commissions for kids in all genres, including interactive and games. She has worked on children's TV and animation at King Rollo Films, Acamar Films, Magic Light Pictures and Aardman, with credits spanning *Fimbles*, *Bing*, *The Gruffalo* and *Room on the Broom*.

Sue Nott

Sue is a freelance Executive Producer and Consultant, specialising in children's and family drama. Recent credits include *The Lodge* (Disney), *Jamie Johnson* (CBBC), *The Worst Witch* (CBBC/Netflix/ZDF) and *Biff & Chip* (CBeebies).

Her producer credits in children's television cover all genres from drama and comedy to documentary and magazine, including BAFTA award winners such as *Coping With Relatives* and *The Ant and Dec Show*. For 18 years she was at the BBC, first as an Executive Producer in Education Production and then as Head of Education for BBC Children's, where she exec'd a wide range of schools programmes from hard-hitting teen drama to preschool puppet shows, and was responsible for the birth of *Tracy Beaker*. Sue was then part of the CBBC commissioning team for 9 years, with responsibility for all independently produced drama including *Eve*, *So Awkward*, *Hank Zipzer*, *Roy* and *Rocket's Island*, as well as helping to establish ground-breaking cross platform dramas *Dixi* and *Secret Life of Boys*.

Cecilia Persson

Cecilia Persson drives an ambitious global strategy for BBC Kids & Family, one of four key Genres that make up BBC Studios Productions. As Managing Director, Cecilia works in partnership with all areas of the business to ensure the most creative, efficient and effective approach to bring children's content to our audiences around the world. Cecilia has extensive creative and commercial knowledge, including more than 15 years at Warner Media, where she most recently held the role of VP Programming & Content Strategy.

Prof Andy Phippen

Andy Phippen is a Professor of Digital Rights at Bournemouth University and is a Visiting Professor at the University of Suffolk in the UK. He has specialised in the use of ICTs in social contexts and the intersection with legislation for almost 20 years, carrying out a large amount of grass roots research on issues such as attitudes toward privacy and data protection, internet safety and contemporary issues such as sexting, peer abuse and the impact of digital technology on wellbeing. He has presented written and oral evidence to parliamentary inquiries related to the use of ICTs in society, is widely published in the area and is a frequent media commentator on these issues.

Nigel Pickard

Nigel Pickard developed and produced a wide range of programmes before becoming Controller of Children's and Family at TVS in 1986. In 1998, he moved to ITV to be Controller of Children's and Youth Programmes, responsible for the commissioning and scheduling of all ITV children's output. In 2000, he was appointed Controller of BBC Children's overseeing the launch of two new channels, CBBC and CBeebies.

In 2003, Nigel was invited back to ITV as Director of Programmes, where his remit was the scheduling and commissioning of the entire ITV output including all drama, entertainment, comedy, factual and religious programmes as well as the acquisition of all films and content from abroad.

After three successful years overseeing major commissions such as *The X Factor*, *Britain's Got Talent* and *Dancing on Ice*, he joined RDF as Group Director of Kids, Family Entertainment and Drama, where, amongst others, he has been responsible for commissions such as *Mister Maker*, *Dani's House*, *Escape from Scorpion Island* and *Tickety Toc* as well as the CBeebies landmark series, *Waybuloo*. After the merger with Zodiak Group in 2010, Nigel assumed the role of CEO MEAA, Zodiak UK Kids.

Nigel is Creative Director, Kids and Family at Nevision. He was a founder member of the Save Kids' TV Executive Committee and became a Board member of The Children's Media Foundation in January 2012.

Gary Pope

Gary began his career as a school teacher and led an English Department before becoming a learning designer for a change management consultancy. A strange internal comms project for Disney led Gary back to children and to launch Kids Industries (KI).

KI solves problems, develops strategies, ideas and products as well as creating content for clients that include Disney, Nord Anglia Education, Pokémon and the BBC. As the only cross-discipline agency that specialises in the family market on the planet, KI uses deep audience insight and 20 years of experience to make children happy, parents satisfied and brands stronger.

Gary has led the design of the multi award-winning subscription product for WWF, built *Peppa Pig's* digital presence globally and led the creation and operationalization of two entire x-platform TV children's channels for Al Jazeera. Gary developed the first HFSS compliant cereal for Kellogg and the Aquafresh range of children's toothpastes. Most recently Gary has led the KI team in the redevelopment of the family offer for Royal Caribbean Cruises – from the proposition to the activities the families enjoy, through to the design of the spaces they use.

Gary's commitment to a sustainable future for families is demonstrated through his position as Children's Ambassador for the Products of Change Group where he advocates for children. Gary is a member of the advisory committee for The Children's Media Conference, a guest lecturer at multiple academic institutions including Oxford and Bauhaus universities, a regular keynote speaker at conferences around the world and a regular industry writer and commentator in mainstream titles. Gary is the recipient of multiple awards for marketing, content creation and strategy including two IPA Strategy Awards and a Webby.

Gary is dad to Daisy and Laurence (and Lucky) and collects Star Wars UCS LEGO. Gary maintains his interest in education as a school governor.

Dr Kruakae Pothong

Dr Kruakae Pothong is a Researcher at 5Rights and visiting research fellow in the Department of Media and Communications at London School of Economics and Political Science. Her current research focuses on child-centred design of digital services. Her broader research interests span the areas of human-computer interaction, digital ethics, data protection, internet and other related policies. She specialises in designing social-technical research, using deliberative methods to elicit human values and expectations of technological advances, such as the Internet of Things (IoT) and distributed ledgers.

Dr Rachel Ramsey

Rachel Ramsey is Associate Director for Research at Dubit, the children and teens-focused research consultancy and digital agency. Rachel recently led State of the Nation, a mixed-method study of young people's feelings and experiences of some of society's greatest challenges. Prior to joining Dubit, Rachel designed and led delivery of the University of Sunderland's research impact strategy, working in partnership with academic colleagues and external partners including the BBC, NHS, British Library and the Home Office to ensure academic research benefits wider society. Rachel has a PhD in cognitive linguistics and has published research on theoretical and empirical linguistics, and on children's language acquisition.

Gemma Robinson

Gemma Robinson studied History of Art at Oxford University before heading into the creative industry, editing design books at Phaidon Press and carrying out curation, sales and research for cultural organisations in the UK. In her role at Thred Media, Gemma consults brands on social change and reaching a Gen Z audience. She also established and now runs the Change Maker Network, a 100+ global community of young activists and journalists.

Mel Rodrigues

Mel Rodrigues is a well respected media practitioner, with 20 years' experience in factual TV production, talent nurturing and D&I.

She recently completed six months as Creative Diversity Lead at Channel 4, working on the channel's new commissioning diversity guidelines, Black to Front project and diverse-led indies fund.

Previous credits include leading the BBC Digital Cities initiative across the UK, training producers for the charity Media Action and producing a large range of network formats in Cardiff, Bristol and London.

In 2019 Mel launched Gritty Talent to design smart and scalable ways to connect under-represented talent into TV. Working with over 40 indies and several major broadcasters, Gritty Talent recently received a commendation at the Edinburgh TV Festival New Voices Awards.

Jessica Schibli

Jessica Schibli is the first ever Head of Diversity & Inclusion for BBC Children's & Education, committed to ensuring that young audiences are reflected authentically in content and ensuring that staff and leadership teams off screen are diverse and inclusive.

Outside of work, Jessica first realised her passion for embedding change and advocating for diversity and inclusion when she set up a forum for under-represented students at the University of Oxford, which has since supported thousands of students. After working in the Finance industry for 15 years, Jessica took up her role at the BBC.

Andrew Snowdon

Andrew Snowdon is Production Manager on *JoJo & Gran Gran* for BBC Studios Kids & Family. He has worked at the BBC for 11 years, with the last 5 years in Children's. He previously worked on CBeebies animation *Go Jetters*.

Peter Stanley-Ward

Peter Stanley-Ward is a Writer/Director and Head of Creative at Treehouse Digital, where he leads a team responsible for international award-winning, Oscar and BAFTA qualifying, short family film *Litterbugs* and hit online series and sequel series *Shelley* and *Shelley 2* for Crypt TV. Most recently he completed the Epic Games supported short film *The Well*.

Prof Jeanette Steamers

Jeanette Steemers is Professor of Culture, Media and Creative Industries at the Department of Culture, Media and Creative Industries, King's College London. Her research interests include media industries, policy and distribution; public service media and children's media. Her work has been funded by the AHRC, British Academy and Leverhulme Trust.

Rebecca Stringer

Rebecca Stringer is the Research Director at KidsKnowBest, leading research in the key behaviours that impact young people's development and helping brands develop global strategies to engage family audiences. Since joining KidsKnowBest Rebecca has worked with brands such as Cartoon Network, eOne, Hasbro, Viacom and LEGO. She is currently completing an MSc at the Oxford Internet Institute studying the social dynamics of the internet, with a focus on young people's experiences.

Garry Vaux

Garry Vaux is a children's book illustrator and author. In 2009 he compiled the first of two books entitled *Legends of Kids TV* after the passing of his mother evoked nostalgia for his childhood. The books included the likes of Simon Farnaby (*Paddington*), Nancy Cartwright (*The Simpsons*), Sir Tony Robinson (*Maid Marion*) and Bernard Cribbins (*The Wombles*) and from that he formed a close friendship with Rick Jones (*Fingerbobs*). In a varied career Garry has previously won awards for graphic design as well as photography. Since 2014 Garry has been a freelance illustrator and has become known for his bright, fun and expressive characters. He's illustrated 21 books to date and is proud to be doing something that he had a love for as a child. Best of all, he can buy copies of *The Beano* and claim it back as a business expense!

Colin Ward

Colin is a lecturer in film and television production at the University of York and Deputy Director of The Children's Media Foundation with responsibility for the CMF's links with the research community. He is a former children's producer and director and started his career at Yorkshire Television, working across factual, entertainment and drama formats. He won a Bafta for *The Scoop* before joining Granada Kids to produce the Bafta-nominated gameshow *Jungle Run*. Moving to the BBC, he won a second Bafta for the gameshow *Raven*, going on to work as an Executive Producer with CBBC Scotland.

Izzy Wick

Izzy Wick is the Director of Policy at 5Rights where she works to put children's needs and rights at the heart of legislative and regulatory proposals and ensure that the same freedoms, protections and privileges that young people are entitled to offline also apply online. Izzy has worked in various organisations across the third sector as well as the Civil Service where she specialised in digital and technology policy and service design.

Dr Ashley Woodfall

Dr Ashley Woodfall worked in television for many years before joining the teaching and research community at Bournemouth University (BU). He is a Fellow of the Royal Society of Arts and the Higher Education Academy. He holds an MA in producing film and television, a PGCE in educational practice and a PhD in children's media engagement, with a primary research focus on children and their media experiences/lives. He is Co-convenor of The Children's Media Foundation (CMF) Academic Advisory Board and a member of the CMF's Executive Group. He teaches undergraduate and postgraduate students media theory and production, with a particular interest in children's and cross-platform media. Ashley is a Senior Principal Academic at BU, having previously been Head of the Department of Media Production and Programme Leader of BA (Hons) Television Production.

Ashley's practice experience includes producing and directing factual, news, continuity, promos, commercials, entertainment and comedy; often with an interactive slant, and mostly within Children's TV. Whilst at Nickelodeon he devised, produced and directed innovative interactive music and game shows. For BBC he created multi-platform content that spanned online, interactive and broadcast. Ashley's career began within MTV and LWT's camera departments, and he still very much enjoys picking up a camera (video or stills) when the opportunity arrives.

The Children's Media
FOUNDATION

Lightning Source UK Ltd.
Milton Keynes UK
UKHW020111240622
404869UK00003B/15